ANGRY
OPTIMIST

ALSO BY LISA ROGAK

*One Big Happy Family: Heartwarming Stories of Animals
Caring for One Another*

Dan Brown: The Unauthorized Biography

*Dogs of Courage: The Heroism and Heart of Working Dogs
Around the World*

*The Dogs of War: The Courage, Love, and Loyalty of Military
Working Dogs*

*And Nothing but the Truthiness: The Rise (and Further Rise)
of Stephen Colbert*

*Michelle Obama in Her Own Words: The Views and Values
of America's First Lady*

Barack Obama: In His Own Words

Haunted Heart: The Life and Times of Stephen King

A Boy Named Shel: The Life and Times of Shel Silverstein

ANGRY OPTIMIST

The Life and Times
of Jon Stewart

LISA ROGAK

Thomas Dunne Books
St. Martin's Press
New York

THOMAS DUNNE BOOKS.
An imprint of St. Martin's Press.

ANGRY OPTIMIST. Copyright © 2014 by Lisa Rogak. All rights reserved.
Printed in the United States of America. For information, address
St. Martin's Press, 175 Fifth Avenue, New York, N.Y. 10010.

www.thomasdunnebooks.com
www.stmartins.com

Library of Congress Cataloging-in-Publication Data

Rogak, Lisa, 1962–
    Angry optimist : the life and times of Jon Stewart / by Lisa Rogak.
        pages cm
    ISBN 978-1-250-01444-3 (hardcover)
    ISBN 978-1-4668-4106-2 (e-book)
  1. Stewart, Jon, 1962–   2. Comedians—United States—Biography.
3. Television personalities—United States—Biography.   I. Title.

PN2287.S683R66 2014
792.7'6028092—dc23
[B]

                                                        2014016493

St. Martin's Press books may be purchased for educational, business,
or promotional use. For information on bulk purchases, please contact
Macmillan Corporate and Premium Sales Department at 1-800-221-7945,
extension 5442, or write specialmarkets@macmillan.com.

First Edition: September 2014

10 9 8 7 6 5 4 3 2 1

For Melanie Vanni, who likes Jon Stewart because
"No matter what's coming down the pike, he's hilarious, he's
commanding, he's E. F. Huttonish . . ."

Also for Seth J. Bookey . . . this book would have turned
out a LOT differently if it wasn't for his judicious help and
persistent and inquisitive eye.

ANGRY
OPTIMIST

INTRODUCTION

Let's get something out of the way from the beginning:

Jon Stewart is a bundle of walking contradictions. On the one hand, he makes no bones about exactly how he feels about things at any given moment, delivering his opinions and thoughts to his audience seriously—usually with an eye toward making them laugh—while also hopefully making them question the way the world works.

On the other hand, he is a man who hides in plain sight. Stewart is an enigma who shuns the spotlight, and his contempt for certain people and philosophies sometimes makes him so enraged on the show that he starts to shake and spit.

"[I'm] a bitter little hairy man of comedy," he has joked.

Actor Denis Leary predicted his friend's progression way back in 1994 during Stewart's first talk show: "Jon's shown more of his nice-guy side so far," he said. "As the show continues, it will get uglier. Eventually it will just be this raging little Jewish man screaming into the camera."

Some days, indeed, that man seems not so far away.

At the same time, the man is comprised of a peculiar mix of anger and optimism, in almost equal proportions.

But the inescapable truth is that Stewart is so damn funny that even the targets of his often caustic observations appreciate his jokes and even laugh at their own foibles as expressed through his eyes.

By his own account, Stewart says he was born with an unorthodox sense of humor that needed to be let out. "I can't remember not being this way," he said. "I can't remember one day thinking, 'You know what might work for me? Humor.' My brother was smart, so there was no way I was going to cop that title in the family, so I naturally gravitated toward another direction of attention: I was the court jester of the family."

At the same time, his humor leans toward taking the side of the underdog.

"He has this internal barometer of what's right and wrong," said Madeleine Smithberg, former *Daily Show* producer. "He has a very sensitive justice meter. He's just way too smart for that little body."

"My comedy is about anything that, when I was growing up, made me feel different or disenfranchised in any way," he explained.

As a result, he developed the tendency to constantly look over his shoulder. "I'm nervous about everything," he admitted.

"Jon is driven by the forces of guilt and shame and fear of being on the outside that give Jews their comic angst," said Ben Karlin, who worked with Stewart on *The Daily Show* for many years.

"Jon is a neurotic nut," added comedy writer Adam Resnick.

Stewart agreed, up to a point. "My comedy is not the comedy of the neurotic," he said. "It comes from feeling displaced from society . . . because we're not in charge.

"But I am probably a lot more critical of things than I should be."

For someone who is so widely adored and respected, Stewart insists that his rise to stardom was unplanned. "People who worry about where they're going next generally don't end up where they think they're going," he said. "When you've got too much of a master plan, it's going to fail.

"As a kid, I never thought, 'I want to be a talk-show host,'" he said. "Some people growing up gazed into the sky and every cloud looked like Johnny Carson. I just wanted to be a good comic. And that was only after I got out of school: 'Well, what do I do now? I like to sleep late and I don't like working.'"

Critics, pundits, and fans all try to parse the man, sometimes from surprising corners—Republican congressman Paul Ryan has called Stewart the funniest man in America while *New York Times* columnist Paul Krugman accused Stewart of "ruining his brand" by dismissing the idea of a trillion-dollar coin—but really, he claims that what makes him tick is pretty simple:

"I think of myself as a comedian who has the pleasure of writing jokes about things that I actually care about, and that's really it," he stressed. "I have great respect for people who are in the front lines and the trenches of trying to enact social change, but I am far lazier than that.

"I am a tiny, neurotic man, standing in the back of the room throwing tomatoes at the chalkboard. When we come to work in the morning we say, 'Did you see that thing last night?' And then we spend the next eight or nine hours trying to take that thing and turn it into something funny."

Regular fans of the show know that in Stewart's eyes, nothing—*nothing*—is sacred. His rapid-fire wit often paints him into corners with people who have every reason to be offended, but luckily they're laughing their asses off instead of being outraged. Stewart was a frequent guest on the Larry King show and he liked to poke fun at the host while pointing out societal hypocrisy and expounding on the current topics of the day.

"We think about all the wrong things rather than solve the problems," he told the oft-married King back in 2004. "And we freak out by gay marriage. I mean, honestly, have you ever been in a gay marriage? I hope I'm not prying."

King's response: "No, I have not."

Stewart: "I just thought, law of averages and all that. I mean, how many out of twenty, how many has it been?"

King: "Stop!"

Stewart: "Ten percent of the country is gay, and you've been married twenty times, so I figured two of them had to be—no?"

Stewart couldn't stop being funny if he tried. After all, his humor has always been fueled by his deep sense of frustration at the injustice, lies, and hypocrisy that are everywhere he looks. "I'm attempting to scratch an itch, and I want to make humor about things I care about," he said. "People always ask, where do the jokes come from? Really, they come from a place of pulling your hair out seeing things that make you cringe and wanting to turn that into something that will make you laugh."

At the same time, he has no tolerance for self-analysis or a *woe-is-me* attitude, which is perfectly understandable since being constantly attuned to something you could feasibly turn into a quick laugh—and ego boost—can't help but turn your view outward, at least when you're in front of an audience.

So when Oprah put him on her couch in 2005 and promptly proceeded to start delving into the cause-and-effect of his life, he quickly waved away her probing questions.

"If you looked at anybody's life, you could find the pain in it and say that what they do is born of that pain," he patiently explained.

But Oprah wasn't done. When she asked if he was teased as a child, he'd had enough, and shot back, *"Who wasn't?"*

But he does admit that his childhood has unalterably shaped his life and sense of humor. "A part of me is probably still trapped in whatever emotional state I was in at fourteen years old, when my nose and head were the same size they are now, but my body was half its weight," he said. "I think there's a part of you that's always stuck in that. And when you look in the mirror, and you evaluate what you're doing, it's always fractionally coming from that perspective."

While other comics with similar physical shortcomings may have woven an entire lifetime's worth of routines around their imperfections, Stewart differentiated himself by steering away from it. Sure, he'll allude to his height and ethnic background every so often, but it's clear he finds it tedious to dwell on them. After all, his is a very specific type of comedy: no pratfalls, no physical pranks. Stewart's brand of comedy emanates 100 percent from his brain.

And he's certainly found the perfect forum sitting behind *The Daily Show* newsdesk. While he will occasionally rail against the iniquities of the world away from his *Daily Show* pulpit, for the most part he keeps a very low profile, and is extremely private and protective of his personal life. Though he will occasionally indulge the paparazzi and allow them to snap a few pictures of himself and his family, photographers know that to camp out on his doorstep in Tribeca would pretty much be a huge waste of time, because once Stewart enters the building after a long day at the studio, he doesn't leave until it's time to head uptown again the next day for the painstaking, pressure-cooker process of putting the next show together. You'll rarely see him mentioned in the gossip columns or read about him partying at some glam black-tie gala.

"I have two speeds in my life," he said, "pedaling a hundred miles per hour uphill to try and stay up, or sitting at home on my couch with a glazed doughnut on my lap staring at a Knicks game. I need downtime to refill the reservoir. I don't have much of a life outside. It is all-consuming.

"I should probably make [my] story interesting, but I got nothing," he said. "I'm trying to imagine Kitty Kelley in here saying, 'Let's do a book' and she'd be in here for five minutes and then she'd say, 'You know what? Screw this.'"

This biographer will tell you that yes, it's been a challenge to research the man. Not only does Stewart keep a low profile whenever he's not toiling away at the *Daily Show* studios, but his friends and colleagues are equally closemouthed about disclosing any quirks or stories about the man. But maybe that's why his audience respects him so much, aside from the acerbic wit, the probing intelligence, and the eagerness to point out hypocrisy: because he's not out claiming space in the tabloids or striving to increase his visibility or Klout Score, they trust him.

He doesn't much care about fame, and indeed, he never set out with grandiose plans for recognition in mind.

"My goal was always to be better than I was at the present time," he confessed.

Yet, despite this laissez-faire attitude, Stewart's always had a backup plan. After all, ever since his father left the family when Jon was ten years old, he's always felt like the rug was about to be yanked out from under him. In yet another exchange on Larry King's talk show, Stewart expressed mild outrage that anyone would consider him as someone who looks on the sunny side of the street.

"I'm a Jew. What kind of question is that, are you an optimist? I always have my bags packed. Is that optimistic? I never know when they're going to knock on my door and [tell me to leave]. There are very few countries that don't have at least one museum going, 'And this is when we chased you out.' That's why we're all in comedy, we want to *stay*."

But it's that same philosophy that has lent a certain degree of flexibility to Stewart's life. After all, while he worked his tail off for years to reach his current level of fame and stardom, his belief—warped though it may be—that it could all disappear tomorrow afforded him an outlook that was all too rare in an industry where many people automatically assumed they were destined to be stars. Of his early days in comedy, he said, "I had to make peace with the fact that if this works, great, and if it doesn't, I had to be okay with that, too. You can't go into it thinking, 'If I do this and they take this away, what's going to happen to me?' You have to know that you can always open an ice-cream store."

And while Stewart may jokingly dismiss any suggestion that he is an optimist at heart—he would never deny the fact that he is indeed at times a very angry man. Yet if he didn't wholeheartedly believe that he could bring about real change for the better in the government, the world, even his own neighborhood, he would have no reason or motivation to work as hard as he has to attract attention to the issues that are near and dear to his heart.

And that is the definition of an optimist in any book.

"The idea that I get to do this for a living is mind-boggling to me," he said. "It really is sort of a dream life."

But that's not how things started out.

CHAPTER 1

When Jonathan Stuart Leibowitz was born on November 28, 1962, in New York City to Donald and Marian Leibowitz toward the end of the huge postwar baby boom, he began a typical middle-class American childhood that was unremarkable for the time, and apparently very much strived for by the majority of people in the United States.

He joined Larry, a brother who was two years older, and the Leibowitz family had little to set it apart from the other families living in Lawrenceville, New Jersey, just down the road from Princeton, in all ways but one. As one of only a handful of Jewish families who lived in the area around the famed Ivy League school—notorious as a well-heeled Protestant college that was rumored to deliberately limit the quota of Jewish students admitted well into the 1970s—the Leibowitzes were determined to live an everyday—and secular—American life in the peaceful heyday of the early 1960s. As Stewart later put it, he never lived anything but a typical American childhood: "I grew up in the good old days before kids had these damn computers and actually played outside."

He watched popular TV shows like *Emergency!* and *The Hudson Brothers Show*, he ate Quisp cereal and collected box tops to redeem for cheap plastic toys, and developed the first crush of his life on Eve Plumb, who played Jan Brady on *The Brady Bunch*.

"My life was typical," he said. "I played Little League base-ball. I never wanted for food. I always had shoes. I had [my own] room. There were no great tragedies. There were the typical ups and downs, but I wouldn't say it was at all sad. We were Jewish and living in the suburbs so there was a slightly neu-rotic bent to it, but I can't point to anything where a boy over-came a tragedy to become a comedian. As my grandmother used to say, 'I can't complain.'"

Despite his apparently normal childhood, young Jon did stand out in one way: he was short. Noticeably so. His class-mates towered above him, and so he made an easy target. And it didn't take him long before he realized the best way to deflect his tormentors was with a witty comment or pointed retort.

"I was very little, so being funny helped me have big friends," he said.

"I realized it was a way of getting attention pretty early on," Jon added. "There was a sense that this feels good, to say some-thing that made everybody laugh. It was a rhythm that made sense to me."

Though the Leibowitzes belonged to a local synagogue and Jon attended a yeshiva kindergarten before moving on to first grade at the local public school, neither parent was particularly interested in immersing themselves wholeheartedly in the Jewish faith. Possibly this was because of a lack of opportuni-ties to do so in and around Princeton, but also because they hoped to distance themselves from their family history and blend into the community more easily. Donald's grandfather was ultra-Orthodox; he ran a shoe store on the Lower East Side of Manhattan and never failed to wear his religion on his sleeve. "When we visited his store, he would . . . make me recite prayers," said Donald. His son—Donald's father—had already begun the move away from a life of extreme religion by becoming a cabdriver in New York. At the time, running a store in an orthodox Jewish neighborhood pretty much ensured that few Gentiles would cross the threshold into the store; on the other hand, a cabdriver gave up control over the types of people he'd interact with over the course of a day.

Marian's family, by contrast, took a more secular route. According to genealogist Megan Smolenyak, Marian's father, Nathan Laskin, was born in Inner Mongolia in 1906 and grew up in Tientsin, China, home to a tiny but thriving community of Jewish entrepreneurs and salesmen, many of whom built thriving businesses as furriers. Most of the settlers had defected from the Russian army after the Russo-Japanese War ended in 1905. According to Marian, Jon took after Nathan, her father, who had a wicked sense of humor and actually subsidized his salary as a fur salesman by moonlighting as a stand-up comic in China in the early part of the twentieth century and later immigrated to Seattle to help expand the business.

Nathan helped run the Manchurian Fur Trading Company before he decided to pull up roots and try his luck at business in the United States. After first landing in Seattle, he eventually moved with his wife, Fannie, and small daughter, Marian, to Cooper Street in Manhattan, where he continued working in the family fur business. In 1940 he pulled in the princely sum of seventeen hundred dollars for the entire year.

After Donald and Marian married in the late 1950s, they

settled into life in Manhattan where Marian worked as a school-teacher and Donald worked at RCA Labs in Princeton, New Jersey.

Shortly after their first son, Larry, was born in 1960, Don and Marian decided to move from New York City to New Jersey to reduce the commuting time to Don's job at RCA Labs. They moved into a house in Lawrenceville, the next town over, about forty miles from Philadelphia. As was typical of the era of the man in the gray flannel suit, mothers held down the fort at home while fathers spent long hours at the office, arriving home often too late to spend time with their children. And Donald was no exception.

The area around Princeton had long leaned toward white Anglo-Saxon Protestantism, and though the Princeton Jewish Center existed, that was about it when it came to Jewish culture in the area. Not only was young Jonathan teased about his height—or lack thereof—but for his name and heritage as well. "Leibotits" and "Leiboshits" were two of the more commonly hurled epithets. "I didn't grow up in Warsaw, but it's not like it wasn't duly noted by my peers that's who I was," he said, adding, "there were some minor slurs." One day in seventh grade he was beaten up by a group of kids while he was waiting for the bus, although he realized that he was at least partly to blame. "I was holding my books and a trellis I had made in shop and thinking, 'How much more of a pussy can I be?'"

Jon took up the trumpet in elementary school and quickly showed that he had a talent for it. He joined a band made up of kids that played big band music with a repertoire that included songs like Glenn Miller's "In the Mood" and Duke Ellington's "Take the 'A' Train." The band of nine- and ten-year-old musicians performed at school and community functions, and also regularly played at a home for juvenile delinquents that is today known as the New Jersey Training School.

In 1971, Jon made his first television appearance ever when the band was invited to play on a children's show known as *Captain Noah and His Magical Ark*, a mainstay children's program on the Philadelphia TV station WPVI that was a must-see for kids in the area. *Captain Noah* was founded by a Lutheran minister who hosted the show along with his wife. Though the show and characters were beloved by parents and children all over eastern Pennsylvania, Jon got his first glimpse of the gulf between what appeared on your TV screen and what happened behind the scenes.

"Captain Noah didn't know anything about kids," said Stewart. "He wasn't a happy guy. You'd see him slide down the slide and say hi to the kids, but there was more to it than that. Essentially, Captain Noah was a mean man who craved a smoke. Those are my memories of breaking into showbiz."

Though in later years Jon would say he had a normal childhood and only learned to develop a keen albeit thinly veiled barbed sense of humor because of his height-challenged stature, the truth is that while those may have been contributing factors, the thing that eventually set him on the path of becoming a comedic star was the direct result of a major tragedy of young Jon's life. After all, it's the rare—possibly nonexistent—amateur or professional comedian who doesn't experience a childhood tragedy—or several—in one form or another.

Jon Stewart was no exception.

To be sure, Donald Leibowitz wasn't overly warm toward his sons or his wife, but that was the norm in an age where fathers worked all day while mothers stayed home and kept house and raised the children. With hardly a kind or encouraging word toward his younger son, Donald had another reason to keep his thoughts and affections to himself: he was having an affair with his secretary. Though it was unclear how long it had been going on when he broke the news to his wife, the Leibowitz family would never be the same.

Back in 1973, when Donald revealed his infidelity and then subsequently moved out, divorce was still a rare-enough occurrence in the United States. Still, after Jon's father admitted to the affair, his parents separated and then divorced.

Ten-year-old Jon was devastated. Marian returned to work as a public school teacher while she and her children learned to manage with less. For instance, when Jon's older brother, Larry, had had his bar mitzvah two years earlier, when the family was still intact, they could afford to spring for a posh celebration and threw an elaborate party at a hotel in nearby Somerville. Jon's bar mitzvah, by contrast, occurred after his father had moved out, when finances were tight. As a result, his coming-of-age ceremony was held at the Princeton Jewish Center, where they also attended High Holidays.

Marian and her sons adjusted the best they could. "She was an anomaly in that era," Jon said. "She had a quiet confidence because she had to fend for herself."

After the divorce was final, Marian, Larry, and Jon got on with their lives. They spent a lot of time with her family, and one of Jon's favorite things to do was to go to the Jersey shore.

"I always loved going there," Stewart said. "When my grandparents were still alive, we would go to Asbury Park. When I was in my teens, we would go to Seaside Heights, or if we thought we could get into a bar illegally, we would go to Wild-wood. If it was a family thing, we would go to Long Beach Island."

But despite the supportive extended family, Jon was often angry, though he tried his best to keep it under control. He was not only mad at his father but at a number of things that were going on in the early to mid 1970s. The area around Lawrenceville in central Jersey was overwhelmingly Republican and conservative at the time, when the rest of the state was engulfed in the protest against the Vietnam War and President Richard Nixon. He grew up during Watergate and Vietnam, and was "infused with a healthy skepticism toward official reports," he said.

He also cut off all contact with his father, refusing to have anything to do with him. Jon's rage was only fueled by his prodigious reading habit, particularly science fiction novels by Kurt Vonnegut and Aldous Huxley.

To avoid getting beaten up, he also worked on developing his sense of humor, in school and out, though he recognized that he had a lot of work to do. "No one has wit at eleven, you're just obnoxious," he said.

By watching and listening to others before coming out with a humorous response, Jon was not only building his own unique style of comedy, he was also in the process of realizing that his own poor view of himself was of his own making. "Those feelings of inadequacy were placed there *by me*," he admitted. "In my own head, I was a weirdo."

But young Jon was a quick learner. In studying various people in order to formulate the funniest reply possible, he soon realized his strengths as well as his weaknesses. For one, it was hard not to feel like he was inadequate when compared to his brother, Larry, who excelled in academics while Jon was an average student who specialized in wisecracks. "I remember being a young kid and seeing him have the Latin Cup from Lawrenceville Prep School, and I just thought, 'Wow! I'm never going to be good enough in Latin to get a cup,'" said Jon. "So I thought I'd better take another route to get attention because, you know what, he's got me trumped on the smarts thing. I took my identity from wising off: smart-ass versus smart."

But he didn't attend Lawrenceville Prep like his brother; instead he entered his freshman year at Lawrence High School in Lawrenceville—other famous alumni at the public school would include Tom Cruise and Michael Eisner—trying not to get beaten up or bullied while learning how his own worldview could make people laugh. Though not all of his teachers would encourage his tendency to crack a joke or be class clown, others encouraged him. According to Larry Nichol, who taught Stewart English in his senior year, "He'd always be saying something on the way out the door as the bell was ringing."

Selma Litowitz, another English teacher, also encouraged her young student. "Jon has said that she was the first who recognized that his humor was something that he could make a living at," said Debra Frank, Litowitz's daughter. Incidentally they lived on the same street. "His joke was that, for many years, he thought that Jews had to live alphabetically."

He always liked sports, and he managed to find one where his small stature wouldn't put him at a disadvantage: he joined the varsity soccer team. The players practiced in all kinds of weather at the fields of nearby Mercer County Community

College. "It would be twenty degrees out and the ground would be frozen solid, and we would be out there running around like idiots," he said, adding that working-class Lawrenceville was more of a soccer town due to the high percentage of immigrant families in town, mostly Italian and Polish. In upper-class Princeton, kids gravitated more toward football.

"I began my sports career as a way out of the suburbs," he admitted. "The best way to describe my ability was to say that after the game the other kids would say to me, 'Way to try!'" Stewart and a friend from up the street spent hours practicing their moves every night, sometimes until midnight. "I spent hours just kicking a ball against a wall, doing anything that would help me get better," he said. "It's always been a part of my personality to be very dogged when I'm unsuccessful."

Though he loved soccer, and was pretty good at it—he actually made the all-state team as an honorable mention—Jon was happiest when pursuing a number of different interests rather than focusing on just one. His tendency toward being a Renaissance man, interested in pursuing everything at least for a short time, blossomed during high school. In addition to playing soccer and being in the school band, he also pursued his desire to work at an incredible variety of jobs, no matter how menial or dangerous. After all, unlike his brother, Larry, who knew he wanted to make his fortune in the financial world, Jon had no idea what he wanted to do and figured he'd try as many jobs as possible in order to check things off his list.

As it turned out, this approach would provide great fodder for a budding comedian. And regardless of the type of work, he could always count on having a new audience where he could pass the time trying to get a laugh out of his coworkers. He took his first job at the age of fourteen in what would become a long string of minimum-wage positions at the Quaker Bridge Mall just outside Trenton; in just over a year, he'd be fired from six different stores at the mall, in some cases because he wanted to make the other employees laugh.

First up: his brother Larry hired him at a department store as a stock boy. Jon gathered up his coworkers and decided to get a laugh the old-fashioned way: with a pratfall into a beanbag chair. Instead of hitting his target, he landed on a display case of aquariums filled with live fish which were soon flopping around on the floor gasping for breath. His mishap resulted in thousands of dollars of damage, and Jon tried to clean up as best he could by disposing of the dead fish into an incinerator, but his brother caught him and fired him before the end of his first day.

But there was another, deeper reason why young Jon made the leap in front of others: he felt like he was born to get in trouble. In fact, he actively pursued any opportunity to test the limits, whether or not there was an audience watching.

"When you feel like you want to express yourself, you need an impetus, a catalyst," he said. "And part of the catalyst is to get yourself in trouble." In addition to being on crutches at his own bar mitzvah because he had broken his ankle playing basketball while on a skateboard, he can rattle off a long list of physical injuries caused by his intentionally trying to get into trouble.

"I'd say 'hey, you see those logs that go up there? I bet I could jump over that.' I went to the emergency room a lot."

Next up: a job as baker's helper and cleaner at a bakery at the same mall. "My job was to wash these huge silver barrels that they made the bread in," he said. "So I would line the barrels with soap and then fill them with water. One day I forgot about the soap and went to scrub tables. Well, the bakery people thought I lined the barrels with flour. Apparently a lot of people found themselves in the mall bathroom that day."

In his senior year, he signed up for the chorus in the annual school musical, *The Pajama Game*, primarily because most of his friends were in it. For one number, the male singers had to wear spats, but since nobody could afford them, they wrapped white tape around their shoes so they'd be visible from the last rows of the auditorium. "Everybody was meticulous about it except me," said Stewart. "I wrapped my shoes up so that it looked like I had an ankle injury or gout. I remember everybody making fun of me."

Later in the show, he decided to make the audience laugh. In a scene in front of a backdrop of trees, the male and female leads were starting to sing a duet where they profess their love for each other, but Stewart had other ideas. In fact, he couldn't help himself. "I wandered out and put my back to the audience and pretended I was relieving myself on one of the trees," he said. "The crowd found this somewhat amusing, the two actors on stage, not so much. I thought, 'Oh, my God, I'm killing. This is awesome! This play is going great.'" While he obviously loved the audience's reaction—and the ego boost that came from making a large group of people laugh—Jon was also beginning to see that there was a time and a place for comedy. "I had to learn when and how to use it, but by God, there's nothing else I could do."

Jonathan Leibowitz
Soupy
College

Stewart's official senior high school year portrait. His nickname "Soupy" could be a reference to comedian Soupy Sales.

He was discovering that he could be powerful through his use of comedy in a way that was impossible in other parts of his life.

"I was obnoxious, and people in New Jersey in the late seventies dug that, man," he admitted. "My role in every social interaction was always as the wisecracking runt who had big friends," he said. "I think that's where I got it. That was my role in the group: basically to get my friends into fights."

In fact, he credits his short stature with helping him to decide to pursue a life of comedy, though it would still be a few more years until he fully committed himself to that career. He theorizes that if he'd even been a few inches taller he's not sure if he would have gone into comedy at all. "I don't know if I would have tried so hard," he said. "I had this vision that life would be peach pies and candy creams if I was six foot two. But if I had been physically bigger, I probably would have wasted even more energy than I did, thinking I was going to make sports my life."

"Those are the makings of a great comic," said Chuck Nice, a fellow comedian. "You're bullied, you're smaller. What you end up doing to survive is to develop a great rapier wit and the ability to make people laugh."

"I think there are virtually no comedians out there who are handsome, well-adjusted, popular, or come from extremely loving, wealthy families," said Devin Gordon, formerly a senior writer at *Newsweek*. "Those people tend not to go into comedy."

Stewart began to study how famous comedians of the time operated, their style, particularly his idols Woody Allen, George Carlin, Steve Martin, and Lenny Bruce. But despite watching them on talk shows, Jon didn't think to aspire to become a talk-show host. "I never watched talk shows when I was a kid and thought, 'Wow, that's a cool thing to do,'" he said. "Like, if I was watching Carson or something I was more impressed with the fact that I was up at eleven o'clock at night."

He was also making his first forays into learning about politics, and testing the waters to discover what his own views were. Before then, he'd only thought about causing trouble. When he was nine years old and traveling with his big band to concerts, he was in a Manhattan hotel room looking down at the street where a van for President Nixon's reelection campaign was parked directly below. "I was thinking, 'If I spit from here . . .'"

Now, though, his ideas were more well-formed. He described himself as being "left-leaning" and "very into Eugene Debs," a union leader and five-time presidential candidate running

BEST SENSE OF HUMOR
Michelle Morrone, Jonathon Leibowitz

Stewart was proud of winning Best Sense of Humor during his senior year at Lawrence High School.

under the Socialist Party banner between 1900 and 1920. During a debate in a high school class, Stewart had to pretend he was Ronald Reagan, at the time a presidential candidate whose worldview and political affiliation was the polar opposite of Debs. "I had to defend my increased military spending," Stewart remembered.

Then, at the age of fifteen, he had his first epiphany about how his life could be different, courtesy of another New Jersey native, Bruce Springsteen.

"The first time you hear *Darkness on the Edge of Town*, you begin to plan how to move out of New Jersey," he said. "When I listened to his music I didn't feel like a loser, I felt like a character in an epic poem about losers. You felt like there was possibility. That here is a guy who grew up like you grew up and had that same feeling of, I bet if I just fucking get in the car and drive, there will be an opportunity for something different and better—an opportunity to be something that I want to be."

And he was starting to think that that "something" involved making people laugh. He was encouraged when he was voted "best sense of humor" in the 1980 graduation class at Lawrence High School.

He hoped that the next four years, which he'd spend at The College of William & Mary in Williamsburg, Virginia, would help him figure that out.

CHAPTER 2

I CAME TO William and Mary because as a Jewish person, I wanted to explore the rich tapestry of Judaica that is southern Virginia," Jon Stewart joked as he accepted an honorary doctorate at the College of William & Mary's 2004 graduation ceremony. "Imagine my surprise when I realized 'The Tribe' was not what I thought it meant."

Though "The Tribe" is often used to describe the Jewish community, in this case at William & Mary, the term was also used as a moniker for the college's athletics department, in the way that other schools use the names of animals like tigers or cougars for their various teams.

William & Mary was founded in 1693, and has long had a reputation as being academically stringent and considered to be one of the "public Ivy League" schools, as it's a state university. Since it's located in Williamsburg, Virginia, far from any significant urban nightlife, social activities on campus relied heavily on Greek life, and the school's racial and ethnic diversity left much to be desired. This is true today as well as when Stewart was a student from 1980 through 1984.

William & Mary at the time was an unusual choice for a Jewish boy from New Jersey: in 2013 the percentage of Jewish students was between 2 and 4 percent, and the student-run Jewish campus organization lacked an advisor, a physical building, and an association with a local synagogue. In 1980, these numbers were significantly lower.

If he felt like an outsider in New Jersey, he was about to get a bigger shock: many of the students Stewart encountered at the college had never met a Jewish person in the flesh before. He was their first. He described them as "boys with eight first names, which also happened to be the names of Confederate generals, but who just went by 'Trip.'"

But Stewart didn't pick the prestigious Southern university for either its academics or religious life: instead, he chose William & Mary so he could play soccer, which was much more important to him than studying and attending classes. He dreamed of playing professional soccer after graduation.

Head coach Al Albert had built a strong nationally recognized men's soccer team at the school, with numerous players going on to pursue successful professional careers after graduation, which would include Scott Budnick, Wade Barrett, and Jeff Agoos. This attracted Stewart's attention.

Plus, following the idea planted by Springsteen, at least it got him out of New Jersey.

Once he was ensconced at the school, his life had an anchor in the form of daily practices and regular games. He started with the junior varsity team as a freshman before Coach Albert invited him to join the varsity team when he became a sophomore. Besides being a starter for the team, he even coached a local boys' high school team at the nearby Gloucester High

Stewart heads off the competition during a college soccer game. *(Courtesy William & Mary)*

School. In fact, it was the first time in his life that he focused on just one activity: soccer. "My years with Tribe soccer were the best of my college experience," he said.

"I didn't know how to be friends with girls; I knew how to hang out with guys in a bus traveling to soccer games, so that was my idea of fun," Stewart continued. "The games were exciting, and there was a lot of passion, and for those ninety minutes it was wonderful."

But it didn't come without a few bumps in the road. "Soccer was a gentlemen's game, and occasionally there were times where the slur would be used," Stewart recounted. "And my last name was Leibowitz and my nose was twice the size of my head, so it was not hard to figure out my ethnic background."

"His overall experience at William and Mary wasn't as positive as a lot of people's," Albert said. "If it wasn't for soccer, he would have left school. But soccer kept him in here. His connection through the school is the program."

He also worked to hone his comic chops on his teammates. "Some of the best people I have ever met, I met down here," he said. "This was the first place I developed my humor."

It was the rare player who would attempt to out-joke him. "Jon's wit was famous within the team," said Albert. "No one would dare even then engage him in verbal combat. None of us imagined he would take things to the level that he has, but he was, even in college, a very funny guy."

"Everybody was . . . afraid of messing with Jon because he was so quick-witted," agreed David Coonin, who played alongside Stewart.

But even he admitted that not everyone appreciated his sense of humor. "[College] was the process where I was somehow trying to hone obnoxiousness into wit," he said. "That is a process that doesn't go easy, a lot of peaks and valleys. In general, William and Mary got more of my obnoxiousness than wit. But I had a great deal of pride in working my way onto the team and becoming a starter. It gave me the confidence that there was a correlation between working hard and success and results and getting better at something."

Despite the rigors of carrying a full course load at a demanding school, Stewart did the bare minimum when it came to academics. Though his initial major was chemistry, he switched to psychology before graduating.

"Apparently there's a right and wrong answer in chemistry, whereas in psychology, you can say whatever you want as long as you write five pages," he joked. "The psychology degree comes from the fact that I was a chemistry major and they kept wanting the *correct* answer, whereas in psychology you basically write whatever you want, and chances are you get a B."

He also joined a fraternity, Pi Kappa Alpha, but ended up resigning after only six months because much of frat life revolved around the enforced bullying of both himself and others, and he had had enough of that during childhood. Unlike then, however, no amount of jokes could deflect the abuse.

"Greek life [offered] a false sense of friendship and was an abusive relationship under the guise of camaraderie," he said. "There are things that are good, but as fun as it was to have parties in that house, it wasn't worth the pressure of living up to someone else's expectations as to what you're supposed to be, and going to meetings where they had parliamentary procedure to discuss a toga party."

After he quit the frat, he moved into a college-owned house at 111 Matoaka Court where the number one rule was, "Don't touch the carpet."

"My college career was waking up late, memorizing someone else's notes, doing bong hits, and going to soccer practice," he said.

He also found time to date and, according to some, had a great deal of success despite his self-consciousness about his height. "Jon was very popular . . . and dated some very attractive women in college," said John Rasnic, who played soccer alongside Stewart and also was his roommate for a time.

At least with some other students Stewart's Jewish background was never forgotten. Teammate Rasnic recalled that a player on an opposing team from Randolph-Macon College, another Virginia-based school, called Stewart a kike. "Jon was

JOHN LEIBOWITZ
Lawrenceville, N.J.

Jon's photo from a soccer program at William & Mary. *(Courtesy William & Mary)*

a little upset, I think, perhaps a bit surprised, but he didn't let it bother him," said Rasnic.

One time, a group of students on an opposing team made a comment about the size of Stewart's nose. Stewart responded that size had never been an issue for him, which elicited a roar of laughter from the crowd and instantly changed the atmosphere.

"From that point on, every time he touched the ball they cheered for him," Albert remembered. "And that was his ability to make people laugh and to win people over without making them agree with him. He was not a polished player and he didn't have the pedigree the other players had, but he had some talent and I think he made the most of the talent he had."

In only two years of varsity play, Jon had developed into such an excellent athlete that Coach Albert invited him to join the U.S. squad of the best young Jewish soccer players from all over the country who were heading to the 1983 Pan American Maccabi Games in São Paulo, Brazil, the penultimate step before the World Maccabiah Games, essentially the Olympics for Jews. The World Games are held every four years in Israel with four different competitive classes including Open, Masters, and Disabled, while the Pan American Games rotated between countries in North, Central, and South America, also every four years.

"When we walked on[to] the soccer field, they called us gringos, they wanted to know if we knew how to play," he said. "After that, they no longer called us gringos."

Stewart's accomplishments over four years of soccer primarily as a midfield defender at William & Mary were prodigious: in addition to scoring ten goals overall, he also made an impression in the 1983 ECAC tournament championship over the University of Connecticut by scoring the winning goal to defeat them 1–0. It was only the second time that the college won the conference championship.

As graduation approached, however, his dream of playing professionally was growing dim. Injuries had plagued Stewart throughout his college career, and toward the end of his final season, he injured his knee to the extent that he was unable to play.

However, despite the camaraderie he felt with the other members of the soccer team, Stewart spent much of his college years feeling like he didn't fit in. And though he continued to use humor as a relief valve, he worried about his future despite his success on the soccer field. "I just didn't know what the fuck I was doing with myself," he admitted. "I was uncomfortable in my own skin, let alone being with kids who were not. So that in itself was probably annoying."

Stewart's senior photo from the 1984 *Colonial Echo*, the William & Mary yearbook. *(Courtesy William & Mary)*

When he received his psychology degree in 1984, he had very little idea what his next step would be.

"When I left William and Mary, I was shell-shocked because when you're in college it's very clear what you had to do to succeed," he said. "You knew what you had to do to get to this college and to graduate from it. The unfortunate yet truly exciting thing about your life is there *is* no core curriculum. The entire place is an elective."

As he saw it, his only choice was to pack up and return to New Jersey.

Once he was back in the Garden State, he picked up right where he'd left off and began adding to the wide variety of jobs that he held in high school.

"I've had an amazing amount of [lousy] jobs," said Stewart.

In 2013, genealogist Megan Smolenyak researched Stewart's ancestral roots for the *Huffington Post*, and what she uncovered about his relatives' diversity of occupations could be used to describe his occupational history precomedy as well. "His forebears have held one of the more eclectic mélange of jobs I've seen," she wrote, "including taxi driver, fruit and vegetable peddler, furrier, shoe store proprietor, and window cleaner."

Though Stewart didn't return to the Quaker Bridge Mall to check off the remainder of the shops and restaurants he could get fired from, he came close.

One of his first postgraduation jobs consisted of testing mosquitoes for encephalitis in the New Jersey Pine Barrens, for which he received the princely sum of $119 a week for the summer. "I had a state car, I'd drive down to the Pine Barrens and think I had the greatest gig in the world," he said. "We'd go out at night and set up these traps and then come back in the morning to [collect them]. Every flying creature in the Pine Barrens would be there."

The traps consisted of giant paper coffee cups wrapped in panty hose which were then attached to car batteries that powered both a light and a fan for each cup. "All the bugs would fly towards it, and they'd get sucked in through the fan and get trapped," Stewart said.

"We'd take them back to the lab and knock them out with chloroform and then sort them out by sex. This would take a while and they would start to wake up." By the end of the summer, he said he looked like he had contracted bubonic plague, though only the female mosquitoes bit. "I had all sorts of chiggers and bites. It was insane."

Once that job ended, he continued on to a local science research lab, and he took a job where his tenure was mercifully short, for obvious reasons: "The scientists would pour radioactive chemicals into beakers and tell me to clean them out," he said.

Next, he took another job working for the state of New Jersey as a puppeteer putting on shows for disabled children with an organization called Kids on the Block. Some of the puppets were disabled, others weren't, and Stewart performed skits designed to help teach kids without disabilities how to relate to kids with physical and emotional issues. "I was a cerebral palsy puppet, a blind puppet, a deaf puppet, . . . and a puppet who couldn't commit to a relationship," he said.

"While the show was a noble effort, it was completely unsatisfying for me. . . . I needed to create something I felt part of."

His desire to make people laugh—on a larger scale than just his teammates or coworkers—was rapidly becoming part of his larger dream. "[The puppet show] was a truly good thing to do, yet I thought, fuck this. I need stand-up," he admitted.

In between nobler jobs such as the puppeteering, he also worked part-time as a bartender at restaurants and bars around Trenton. The irony wasn't lost on him. "I was literally helping and hurting people, all on the same day," he said.

But he still had to make a living, so he ditched the puppet gig and ramped up his bartending gigs, driving an "off-brown" Gremlin back and forth to work while listening to his beloved Bruce Springsteen on the car stereo. The Bottom Half was the name of one bar, tucked into a windowless basement below a liquor store in Trenton; City Gardens, an alternative rock club, was another. Jon gladly worked shifts there since popular bands like the Ramones and Butthole Surfers played often, and in fact Joey Ramone became a regular customer.

He enjoyed the work, the music, and clientele, and even invented a drink called A Whack in the Head, combining a Long Island Iced Tea with an Alabama Slammer. "Drink two, and you're not getting up the stairs," he joked.

But despite his work and social life—he also played on a local softball team every spring—Stewart still felt like he was on the outside looking in, wondering why everyone else seemed so much more happier than he felt.

"When I tended bar, I was always happier behind the bar, not out rocking to the band," he said.

In a way, he equated bartending with his glory days as a college soccer player.

But the stress of cutting off drunks and watching other people have the time of their lives night after night took a toll. He decided he would be happier back at a more conventional job, and so hung up his bartending apron and once again took a job working for New Jersey state government, landing a position in the disaster planning preparedness department.

Because he happened to be proficient at a new database program known as Lotus 1-2-3, he was assigned to make lists and keep figures on state resources.

"I made charts . . . in case we were attacked by Pennsylvania," he said.

As usual, he was good at his job and his supervisors and managers loved him, but inside he just felt dead. He wanted to start doing something he felt was worthwhile along with developing his own identity—hopefully one that involved making people laugh, the only thing that made him feel normal, like he belonged—and so he weighed his options.

"I was a little lost from the age of eighteen to twenty-four," he said. "I was . . . working for the state and playing on a . . . softball team . . . thinking, this is it for the next seventy years? I realized that if I didn't watch it, I'd be forty and this would be me, but instead of playing softball, I'd be the guy organizing the team.

"Plus, they were about to re-up me for another forty years [at my job], and . . . I'm twenty-three. . . . I can *always* be one of the bitter guys in my town. It's not like they won't save a seat for me.

"Besides, I'm way too young for a dental plan," he joked.

So he made his decision. Though he had shared with a few people his dream of making audiences laugh for a living, to his friends and family it still came as a shock when he broke the news. He had kept it mostly secret because he didn't want anyone to discourage him or talk him into a life that included a safe bet: a job with the state, insurance, pension, the works.

"I'd never told my friends or family . . . so to them it was like a bombshell."

But to him, it was the only thing that made sense. When watching comedy, he thought, "That's how my brain works," he said.

"[I became a comic] because I was uncomfortable in other settings. . . . As bad as I was when I started, it still felt better than anything else I'd ever done."

"When he finally decided to become a comedian, it was a little bit of a shock," said his mother, Marian Leibowitz. "But he was going to New York, he wasn't going to China. I decided I wasn't going to be the person to discourage him."

Stewart packed a bag, found a place to sublet in Manhattan, and left for New York City. "I threw everything away and moved to New York on a six-week lease," he remembered.

As usual, on the seventy-mile drive, Jon turned to his role model for a little boost in confidence. Years later, he'd tell Bruce Springsteen on *The Daily Show* how important his music was to helping him get on that very soundstage. "You go through the tunnel, take a chance, and you can work to get away from your circumstance. And by working to get away from your circumstance you can make something better of yourself, but there's no guarantee. But you know what? The joy of it is chasing that dream, and that was my inspiration for leaving New Jersey and going to New York. So I just wanted to thank you personally from the bottom of my heart for giving me something to put into the dashboard as I drove a U-Haul van through the Holland Tunnel."

CHAPTER 3

In 1986, Jon Stewart risked everything to move to New York City to pursue his dream of becoming a stand-up comic.

He had a small problem. After he settled into city life, it took him almost a year before he worked up the courage to go onstage in front of an audience for the first time. Of course, every budding stand-up comic needs time to prep, to develop a routine, to study every word and nuance of routines by the greats, but Stewart had another issue to face. He had never actually performed comedy onstage. The closest he'd come was his prank in the musical during his senior year. He was at a clear disadvantage compared to the seasoned comedians who went from one open mike to another in the course of an evening.

While he had plenty of experience cracking jokes with his friends or while standing behind the bar, Stewart had never told jokes onstage.

He was understandably terrified.

"I was in the city for a good nine months to a year before I had the balls to go up onstage," he admitted.

So while he worked up the courage to walk through the

doors of a comedy club that held regular open mikes where anyone could tell a couple of jokes at least for a few minutes before getting heckled off the stage, Stewart continued his habit of working odd jobs: driving a catering truck to deliver food to fancy events around town or busing tables at a Mexican restaurant, all while listening to Lenny Bruce records in his off hours. He had a vague notion that if comedy didn't work out after a while, he'd apply to law school.

After months of putting it off, in the fall of 1987 he finally worked up the nerve to walk into the storied Bitter End on Bleecker Street on a Monday night at one o'clock in the morning and get up onstage. Woody Allen and Bill Cosby had gotten their starts at the Bitter End, so he thought he would be in good company. Besides, the audience would be sparse at that hour, so he wouldn't have to worry about getting heckled off the stage.

He was wrong. "Everybody's first song, first joke, is 'This is who I am, this is where I was raised, this is who my parents are,'" he said.

But first, the host botched "Leibowitz" during his introduction, which was a bit of a surprise in a city filled with seemingly unpronounceable names, Jewish and otherwise. It obviously didn't help his nerves.

So he took a deep breath and told his first joke on his first-ever attempt at stand-up:

"It's lunchtime in the Diamond District," he told a scattered crowd of drunks, tourists, and combative and competing comics. "All the stores close down and the street is filled with chasidim, who suddenly find themselves caught in Yidlock."

He was met with crickets before the heckling started.

He gamely continued with more jokes in the same vein, about being Jewish in New York—though he had been warned by another club owner that this being New York, they didn't need any more Jewish comedians—and approximately three minutes after he began, a guy in the audience yelled, "You suck!"

"Jon went up on stage and bombed," said Paul Colby, who owned the Bitter End. "I mean he bombed atomically. It was terrible to watch. By the time his set was over, Jon had had quite enough of show business. He said good-bye, vowing never to go near a stage again."

But Wendy Wall, Colby's assistant, ran after him as he high-tailed it out of the club, head down, face burning with shame. "I wouldn't say he bombed," she said. "It was one [A.M.]. It's not easy with a crowd like that."

In any case, Wall saw something in Jon, a spark in between the Jewish jokes and the struggle not to visibly cringe at the heckling. She pulled him aside for a quiet talk and encouraged him. Part of him didn't believe her, but a tiny part did. She actually made him promise her that he'd come back and give it another shot. Though it took him four months before he worked up the nerve to grace the stage again, he did, because despite the harassment and anxiety, telling jokes to an audience made him feel "better than anything else."

So he took the stage again at the Bitter End for another open mike—with Wendy Wall standing off to the side to encourage him—but before he gave the emcee his information for the introduction, he did something different.

He changed his name. Instead of Jon Leibowitz, he became Jon Stewart, using his middle name as his surname, altering the spelling.

"Most people assume I changed it because it was too Jewish, but I've never shrunk away from that. Half my act is devoted to being Jewish," said Stewart. "It was something I needed to do. My folks got divorced. I was re-creating myself. It was a symbolic change. I was at a weird point in my life. At the time, I was really searching for a way to get away, to push a different path. I had lost my job, lost my girlfriend, and moved to New York on a lark. I have no regrets about it."

"The host's hesitation at trying to pronounce my name that first night bothered me," he said years later. At the same time, even though Jewish jokes would become part of his stock in trade over time, he didn't want the joke to be on *him*. "You don't want a tauntable handle in show business." But even more than that, he admitted that some of the reason behind his decision to change his name came from "some leftover resentment at my family." In other words, his father.

Things went better for him the second time, and he quickly delved into new routines, polishing snappy comebacks to the hecklers, and more importantly, winning the respect of club owners around the city. While he continued to work at the Bitter End, he also started to appear at the Comedy Cellar, another notable stand-up club, where he soon took the last gig of the night five nights a week, which started at two in the morning.

"I was the last guy [to go onstage] on weeknights," he said. "I wasn't good enough for weekends. But at 1:45 A.M., I went up there and did whatever popped into my head."

For his routines that first year he combined the subjects of religion, media, and politics and how he felt about them—similar to what he ended up doing with *The Daily Show* years later—but admittedly his material was much less polished and aware.

"As I went on every night, I learned the difference between impersonating a comedian and being a comedian," he said. "That was my break, learning how to be authentic, not to the audience, but to myself. I developed a baseline of confidence and also insecurity. I knew how bad I was, and I knew how good I was. And that is what helped me through a lot of the ups and downs as we went along.

"It took me six years to write my first forty-five minutes," he admitted.

For the first year he spent in New York, he continued to work at a variety of menial jobs to pay the rent, but once he won the Comedy Cellar gig, he took a job with the City University of New York as a contracts administrator so that he could spend his evenings traveling from one club to another to check up on the competition and study their routines before heading to his own regular gig.

And what competition it was. Ray Romano, Chris Rock, and Louis C.K. all started around the same time, along with Adam Sandler. For the most part, Stewart was at least a few years older than the rest of them.

"I remember thinking at the time—and these were my exact thoughts—'These young punks are going to have no trouble at all making it big, and that's really annoying,'" he said. "You could just see success on Adam, even back then."

They began to hang out together, riffing off of each others' hang-ups and visiting comedy clubs as a group. Stewart learned that they all shared the same traits: that while they weren't the most optimistic people in the world, there was something about comedy that helped ease their pessimistic worldviews.

"Most comedians are incredibly cynical," said Stewart. "They do it to feed something in themselves. Somewhere in their brains a neuron fires happily and a need is eased, like a drug. It's almost self-medication."

Most comedy clubs in New York paid either in "carfare," ten or twenty bucks, or a meal. Stewart didn't care. "I used to trudge around to four clubs a night, working for falafel money," Stewart admitted.

Stewart was fortunate in his timing: live comedy was becoming more popular at the time, and when he first started pursuing the life of a stand-up comic, demand was at an all-time high. New clubs were opening every week around the country, and restaurants and entertainment venues launched "comedy nights" on a regular basis. Open mikes in major cities like New York and Los Angeles were regularly scouted by talent agents and producers looking for the next best thing, and even in smaller regions, aspiring comics still held out hope that they could be discovered.

"You could travel the country and make six hundred bucks, eight hundred bucks a week, or you could do what I was doing, which was open mikes for a plate of falafel."

He decided to stay in New York, work his day job, and play the clubs at night. Besides, he was still learning what material worked best.

"The hope was just to get better, to learn what your voice was," he said. "It was, in some respects, an exercise in Outward Bound for neurotics. It was a mental challenge. I honestly think it was a rhythm that I didn't realize that I had. Until I got onstage, it didn't actually make sense."

Because he had never performed in front of an audience before landing in New York, he learned in a trial-by-fire way that making your friends laugh is worlds away from making an audience of occasionally hostile, often drunk strangers laugh.

But that's taking the easy road to comedy.

He also honed his ear. "In a weird sense, comedy is a lot like music to some extent," he said. "You use your ear, you hear the flat notes, and do your best to try to avoid them. It's an intuitive process, and your barometer is internal. And due to the volume of what we do, you hit a lot of flat notes, but it's your gut that tells you what to proceed with."

He was thrilled at everything he was learning, and there was a part of doing stand-up that reminded him of being back behind the bar, serving drinks and holding court for his audience.

"When I first got into it, it was sort of like bronco riding: how long can I stay up here? But there's an excitement of being uncensored and just speaking your mind. It's one of the most exciting raw kind of forms of [performing] because you're out there every night. In some ways, it's gladiatorial.

"You come to the realization that the special part is the moment of creation, and the rest of it is maintenance. When you take an act out and do it eight times in four days, you're not gonna come up with much new stuff and it's probably gonna become tiresome. Not only for you, but the waitstaff. You always hate it when the bartender is mouthing your punch lines. And not in a happy way."

He also learned that stand-up was different from one night to the next, and there was no use beating himself up over reacting to the extremes.

At the same time, however, despite the encouragement he received from audience members, club owners, and other comedians, he constantly doubted himself and his abilities. His stress levels were through the roof.

"It was a very anxious time," he admitted. "It was really a

matter of, 'Who am I and what am I doing?' I thought of stopping every day for the first four years."

"The first two years it was a constant battle," he added. "I almost quit halfway through sets sometimes. It's really frustrating. I mean until you get your legs, you don't even know what you're doing. Don't forget, it's not like you're playing the Taj Mahal. It's more like Uncle Fuckers Chuckle Hutch and everybody's hammered."

"When he first started, Jon used to express a lack of confidence in himself," said Noam Dworman, owner of the Comedy Cellar. "But then very quickly he became a very strong act. And then at some point he began to feel it was obvious he was heading for something bigger."

Stewart soon discovered that comedians with self-esteem far higher than his own quickly folded in the face of heckling and criticism. He began to see that the fact that he didn't give up was just as important as honing his craft and studying the routines of others.

"Basically you write jokes and those that work you keep doing and those that don't, you throw out," he said. "I wish I could say there was a magic formula, but I just kept working at it."

Stand-up veteran Chuck Nice agreed. "Perseverance is key, because you will get your chance in this business if you stick it out," he said. "When I first started doing comedy, I ran into a famous comedian and asked, 'What can you do to make it in this business?' And he said, 'Stay in the game, just stay in the game.'"

Indeed, that's exactly what happened for Stewart. A little over two years after he first took the stage at the Bitter End, Stewart was able to quit his day job and live off what he earned telling jokes to total strangers in front of a brick wall in a basement in Greenwich Village.

Despite his success, his anxiety was never far from the surface. Once he had some experience under his belt, he auditioned at a club on the Upper East Side called the Comic Strip Live that was known for helping to launch the careers of Billy Crystal, Eddie Murphy, and Jerry Seinfeld. But the manager gave him a thumbs-down. "I was so gun-shy about it that I never went back there, even after it was working for me," he said. "It was sort of like being a kid and being scared by a mop because you thought it was a monster, and now you have this weird thing about mopping."

Another time Stewart was booked for a show and he was sorely tempted to quit stand-up afterward. He was the opening act for musician Dave Mason at the South Street Seaport in lower Manhattan. "There must have been a thousand people there and halfway through the set, I realized that none of them were facing me," he said. "Instead, they were all looking at this naked guy who was dancing around. At a concert that's far more interesting than a guy talking about his grandmother."

Stewart decided to hit the comedy circuit on the road to test the waters and see how it compared with the New York comedy scene. He didn't stay long. Not only did his Jewish shtick not travel well in some locales, but the lifestyle itself was less than desirable.

"People don't realize how fucking boring it is to go to a town outside Detroit from Tuesday to Sunday and stay in a Ramada Inn until seven o'clock at night," he said. "I remember when I first went on the road. I'd go to a place like Lubbock, Texas, and ask, 'What do you guys have, a prairie dog museum? I'm there.'

You explore every inch of that town, and by three years into it, you could be doing a gig in the Vatican and be like, 'Nah, I'm not going out. I'm fucking staying in my room and drinking.'"

In addition to staying in motels, comedy clubs would often put visiting comics up in apartments and condos solely for their use. "I've stayed in comedy condos that had huge holes in the walls because the last comic there didn't have as pleasant a time as he'd expected," he recalled.

Stewart had become friends with another stand-up comedian, Lizz Winstead, and they shared the same dim view of constantly touring from one comedy club to the next. "Stand-up has become a giant nightmare," she said. "The only comics who are working the road consistently are really blue and pretty low common denominator."

And so he settled back into Manhattan where one of his roommates turned out to be future (and now former) New York congressman Anthony Weiner. They hung out in the same circles when Weiner worked for another former New York congressman-turned-senator, Chuck Schumer. One of Weiner's coworkers had played on Stewart's soccer team at William & Mary, and Weiner had been dating another of Stewart's roommates. Eventually Weiner moved into their Soho apartment and they also shared a beach house together. "It was a classic New York [situation]," said Weiner. "We were all making twenty grand. I was living there more or less because I was bumming off of my girlfriend who was living there."

As Stewart continued his stand-up career, it didn't take long for TV to start calling. In 1989, he heard from a producer for *Caroline's Comedy Hour*, a new show on the fledgling A&E network that basically broadcast stand-up routines from Carolines on Broadway. The comedy club by Caroline Hirsch had been launched in 1981 in New York and attracted top-tier comics from the very beginning, primarily because she paid them.

"Carolines was different in that it was an actual job," said comic Gilbert Gottfried.

Though Stewart had previously performed onstage at Carolines, Hirsch had other ideas for him. Like Wendy Wall, Hirsch said she saw something different about Stewart from the very beginning. "It's not easy, it takes a while, because you get to see that person and you think that person has a little something, but that doesn't mean they all develop," she said. "They have to work hard at it and morph." She put him to work, after she moved the club to a bigger space at the South Street Seaport in downtown Manhattan, doing a children's show, where a handful of comedians who regularly performed uptown did a show for kids. "Stewart was a Captain Crusader type, a superhero with a cape."

She also hired him for the new TV show. Stewart started as a writer for *Caroline's Comedy Hour*, penning segues between stand-up segments as well as TV-friendly routines for some of the visiting comics. He also performed his own stand-up routines on a few occasions.

He also began to work on a show called *The Sweet Life* on a small cable channel known as HBO's Comedy Channel, which would later morph into Comedy Central. The variety show starred singer Rachel Sweet, who hosted a wide range of guests—famous and otherwise—in between comedy scenes and sketches. When that show went off the air after two years, Comedy Channel executives put him to work in front of the camera on a sketch-comedy show called *Short Attention Span Theater*, where he served as cohost with actress and comedienne Patty Rosborough. The premise of the show was simple: in between showing snippets from stand-up comic routines and films currently airing on HBO and Cinemax—which along with Comedy Channel were both owned by the Home Box Office parent corporation—Rosborough and Stewart would offer up commentary and jokes on the clips. Essentially, the show existed as a promotional vehicle.

Stewart hosted the show for two years before MTV tapped him to serve at the helm of *You Wrote It, You Watch It*, a show where viewers would send in ideas for comedy sketches which would then be acted out by Stewart and a group of actors in an ensemble called The State.

You Wrote It, You Watch It went on the air in 1992 but it lasted only thirteen weeks before MTV pulled the plug. As Stewart later described the show, "It was an odd cross between a reality-based show and a sketch show," he said. "[When I was] offered the job, my agent said, 'Take it. It's stupid but it'll be good for your career.' I didn't understand then, but she was right."

The sketches were pretty abysmal in their content, by Stewart's own estimation, with topics ranging from passing gas to a woman who was laughing so hysterically that licorice inexplicably shot out of her nose.

"You should see the ones we didn't use," said Stewart. "We got scads and scads of letters about people vomiting on animals."

After the show was mercifully put out of its misery, Stewart got the break he was dreaming of: he was booked to perform a stand-up routine on *Late Night with David Letterman* in March of 1993.

"When I walked onstage, I blanked," he said. "The audience is dark, and there's just a little red light. [I] realize[d], it'll be *really* quiet here if I don't talk.

"And afterward, my sit-down with Letterman was like an audience with the pope."

"It's a great stepping-stone in the career of any comedian," said Caroline Hirsch. "You get on there and do six minutes of stand-up and sit and talk with Dave, and you get asked back on again. And the more you're on TV, the more you're known and you become a bigger star."

With the applause still ringing in his ears, reality sunk in shortly after Stewart left the studio. "I had a great time and it felt really great, and afterward I went home to my illegal sublet," he recalled. "It was a lesson that this whole life is a journey. There is no such thing as 'made it.'"

He was so excited about his debut that he even reached out to his father, who he had not been in touch with since leaving New Jersey. However, Stewart's earlier decision to change his name was cemented when he heard his father's reaction to his TV appearance: "I always thought they picked more experienced people."

Going on *Letterman* not only provided him with increased recognition from the public, but also among producers and industry people who started to think he deserved his own audience and could carry a show by himself. A few short months after his debut, Letterman announced that he'd be leaving NBC and taking his show to CBS, and so NBC started to look for a show and host to replace him. The candidates were eventually winnowed down to Stewart and Conan O'Brien, who had little experience in front of the camera and was known primarily as a writer on *Saturday Night Live* and *The Simpsons.*

To everyone's surprise—including his own—O'Brien got the job despite having only about "forty seconds" of on-air experience, as he put it.

"It's the worst feeling in the world to think you are going to get a vehicle and see it go to someone else," said Chuck Nice. "That can really demoralize you."

But Jon didn't have long to mourn the missed opportunity. As it turned out, MTV hadn't forgotten about him. Plus his close brush with almost getting the NBC gig had instantly elevated him in the eyes of television producers. MTV was beginning to branch out by making shows that offered more than just compilations of music videos. They were specifically looking for someone to host a talk show who had just the right balance of hipster cool and snark, who could appeal to people in their twenties who were already faithful viewers of MTV.

Despite the fact that he was thirty years old, Stewart fit the bill perfectly in all other ways, and *The Jon Stewart Show* debuted in the fall of 1993.

CHAPTER 4

W<small>HEN</small> *T<small>HE</small> J<small>ON</small> S<small>TEWART</small> S<small>HOW</small> debuted on MTV on October 25, 1993, it was entering an already crowded field. Just as the market for stand-up comedy was growing when Stewart first entered the fray, when his half-hour show launched, it was part of a talk-show boom that was going on, with actors including Ricki Lake, Chevy Chase, Vicki Lawrence, and Arsenio Hall all offered their own shows.

"There are four other talk shows battling it out out there, and we think Jon is the best shot we can take in that environment," said Doug Herzog, who served as president of MTV Productions at the time. "Plus, Jon has that MTV attitude. He has a hip, skewed way of looking at things and, even though he can act like a wise guy, he's also very sweet."

Both Stewart and MTV executives knew they were going after an audience that was different from the other mainstream network talk shows that were hitting the air at the time, and to clinch the deal, the network scheduled his show to come right after *Beavis and Butt-Head*, an animated series starring two teenage miscreants whose favorite activity was to sit on a couch while watching music videos and make typically teenage comments about them. From the time the first episode aired in the spring of 1993, the cartoon was a hit, garnering a large audience of teenagers and twentysomethings, the target audience for Stewart's show.

"This show is a little bit more seat-of-the-pants than what people are used to seeing on network television," said Stewart. "Anything unpredictable is usually miraculous and much better than what you could have planned."

"Imagine if you sit there and you've seen three morons in one hour: Beavis, Butt-head and me."

"We didn't sit around wondering, 'How do we make a Generation X talk show?' It just represents my sense of humor," said Stewart. "How I am on the show is how I am, except, of course, that I'm miked."

One look at the set and it was clear this wasn't a typical talk show of the early 1990s. The stage set looked like it came from the back of a grubby auto mechanic's garage, while the several black-light panels serving as backdrops were nice touches in keeping with the overall industrial theme. Stewart used a wooden tabletop hockey rink—known as Nok Hockey—for his desk, and guests perched on the front seat of an old car that had been pulled from a junkyard.

"We're a little more casual than some of the other programs," he added. "The pressure isn't as harsh. People can check in and hang around. Other shows are very much in a war. We still have that annoying puppy-type quality of just being happy to be here."

He also realized that if the program was on a more widely watched network, then he would be running a very different show. "If we were doing the show on network, we'd probably have to rein it in a little bit. We can be rougher and it doesn't appear out of place because of the context of the channel we're on."

Case in point was when model Cindy Crawford appeared on the show. After he told her she had very soft skin, she pulled a vial of skin cream from her purse and proceeded to apply it to the top of his hand. When she asked him if it felt good, he replied, "I don't know, Cindy, when I have cream on my hands, it's usually on the other side."

In any case, he admitted he preferred being on MTV because he wasn't required to put on airs. "The way I dress on the show, that's what I like, that's how I live, except the show is cleaner," he said. "If it were really my life, it would be me and the guest and a pile of dirty laundry next to us. And some cat litter that needs to be changed."

Improbably, given the juvenile lead-in show, MTV believed Stewart would be able to attract a female audience to the show. "Women will love him as well, which is important because we see this as having broad appeal," said Herzog. "He's perfect for MTV without being too MTV."

"We were an aberration on MTV," said Stewart. "We actually talked to people seven minutes at a time."

The cable channel committed to twenty-four episodes, and Howard Stern was the first guest. His book *Private Parts* had just been published and he was booked on the show to promote it. Stewart was a big fan and he spent hours planning his responses to every possible retort. But the interview didn't get off to a great start.

"I don't know who you are and you're going to be off the air in six weeks," said Stern. He then proceeded to criticize Stewart while the brand-new talk-show host tried valiantly to hide his shock. "Howard was just nailing me left and right, so I did the only thing I could do. I just flipped open his book and I go, 'What's this chapter on lesbians?' Woo. He was off me."

With Conan O'Brien making his debut on NBC around the same time, it was natural for critics to compare the two shows. By and large, they preferred Stewart's approach and style as more refreshing.

"Conan's show was billed as the voice of Generation X, so there was that expectation, but I don't think he cuts it," said *Entertainment Weekly* TV critic Bruce Fretts. "Conan's show feels so forced, like they're trying so hard to be hip and ironic."

And compared with the other talk-show competitors at the time, Stewart's show stood out for its length: it was thirty minutes while the others were an hour or more. "The whole point [is] that even when it sucks, it's only a half-hour," said Stewart. "So come on, they can sit through that. If they can sit through a half-hour of a Flowbee commercial, they can certainly sit through a half-hour of my show."

From the start, the bulk of guests were bands with music videos currently on heavy rotation on MTV, which made sense given who was footing the bill. "It was important to get people the MTV audience recognized." But at least Stewart had a passing familiarity with the bands and so could hold a halfway interesting conversation with guests.

"The bands we have on the show play the music I listen to," he said, but as for the nonmusical guests, given that he was on a cable channel with little to no budget, he essentially had to book B- and C-level stars who were already in New York. "The guests are more of a potluck of who's in town," he said. "Letterman sits down to feast, and then we ask, 'Are you gonna finish that?'"

That said, some higher-caliber celebrities did appear on the show from time to time. Both Cindy Crawford and William Shatner visited and Stewart made an effort to convince some of the stars from *The Brady Bunch* to come on the show. But he quickly learned that the best approach to the show was to essentially wing it, instead of scheduling it down to the second.

"You can't plan this kind of show in advance," he said. "We spent four months designing the show, and the first week we were on the air it was evident that seventy-five percent of the stuff we thought would work didn't."

The late Anna Nicole Smith also made an appearance, and her constant drug-addled state provided Stewart with a bit of amusement. "I was used to viewers falling asleep during the show, but this was the first time we had a guest do it," he said. "I'd ask a question and then she'd begin to *try* to answer. About halfway through it she asked, 'What was the question?' When we went to commercial—I had never seen this before—she had an Indy pit crew with her. All of a sudden eight guys come out and twist her head and slap her around, and there's one lady in the front going, 'Come on, you can do this.' We came back and she was a little fresher."

Finally, after years of working the wee hours at clubs all over the country in front of drunks and hostile people, he could relax . . . a little. Plus, he started to be recognized in public.

"It's completely weird," he said. "I was at this Denny's in

New Jersey at two thirty in the morning, and a bunch of kids home from college spotted me. They were like, 'Wow! What are you doing here in Denny's, man? You're on MTV!' They just were so exuberant, it really blew me away."

After years of obscurity and still getting booed regularly, it was taking a little bit of time to adjust to television fame.

His increased visibility put him in demand in other entertainment venues. Now that he had a TV show of his own—albeit on a cable channel—other talk shows clamored to book him as did some of the comedy clubs that had blown him off when he was unknown. Hollywood also started to consider him for movies.

And he started to phase out a vision of his future being a miserable existence that he had carried around for years: "The prophecy I'd created for myself was one room without a bathroom, [where I was] a miserable old guy who will never love or be loved."

With his fortunes rising, he was able to upgrade from his cramped studio apartment—it was so small that, in his words, he could "touch all four walls while perched on the toilet"—to a one-bedroom in Greenwich Village. He could have moved to a much larger apartment in a more expensive neighborhood, but the experience of his parents' divorce and the financial challenges that followed were still fresh in his mind: the rug could be yanked out from under him at any moment. So he decided to play it safe.

"This is a business built on quicksand," he said. "But I'm trying to get more perspective and allow myself to enjoy things. Occasionally, I'll think, gee, this really is a lot of fun.

"It's the little things in my life that have changed," he said.

"I don't have to worry any more about taking a cab or buying a new CD." Always an animal lover, he brought his two cats with him, one of which was blind. It took the cat a while to adjust to the new accommodations. "He kept walking into the walls, poor guy."

He also thought his luck with women would improve once he got his own TV show—especially since a number of models, actresses, and even *Playboy* Playmates appeared on the show. "They come on, I feed them cheese, and they go, 'Well, thanks a lot. I have to go now and have sex with a big construction worker–looking guy.'"

To his great dismay, the reverse actually happened, and he referred to his love life as stunted. "I'm finally in a position where women would find me more appealing, but I don't really have that much time," he lamented. "I'm basically really isolated, 'cause I work on the show all the time. And it's sort of boring. A career is a lovely place to hide from your social life," he said, adding that the top qualities he looked for in a woman were "compassion and a sense of joy."

But even if he wanted to pursue women romantically, it was clear that they often regarded him in a different light. Once, after actress Tawny Kitaen appeared on the show, she revealed her true thoughts about Stewart. "You want to take Jon home with you, like a puppy," she said.

He also discovered that hosting and planning four shows each week was worlds away from showing up at a nightclub, doing a twenty-minute routine, and then maybe having a beer with the other comics before heading back home or to a lonely motel room, with pros and cons all around.

"For me, coming from the comedy clubs, this is a very

relaxed atmosphere," he said. "Nobody's drunk. It's not one o'clock in the morning. I don't have to shout. Everybody seems to be listening. It's a really good environment."

On the other hand, there was a great deal of stress involved. His anxiety levels went through the roof and he became sick so often that around the studio his nickname was Susceptible Boy. "My respect for the guys who [host talk shows] has risen dramatically since I've tried to do it," he said. "There's a lot to keep in mind while you're out there."

After all, Stewart was now directly responsible for a full staff. "I try to give as much preparation as I can," he said, "but there's a lot of other things that I have to worry about, not only the comedy but also the fact that we tape two shows in the course of one day, which sometimes puts us behind the eight ball."

There was another issue that Jon never had to worry about onstage at the clubs: his appearance. He now had to select his wardrobe with an eye toward his audience and sit in a chair before each taping while a makeup artist did her stuff. "You don't want to see him without makeup," a *Daily Show* employee would say years later. "He's not just sallow, he's the color of a manhole cover."

"They have to shave my neck . . . between tapings," Stewart admitted. "Is that something I shouldn't have shared?"

But overall, both host and guests didn't get too worked up over the specifics. Given the informality of the set as well as the age of the demographic, a certain lack of style was the rule. "We could have the conductor of the Philharmonic on, and he'd be wearing overalls," said Stewart. "I think everybody takes one look at me and says, 'Okay, this guy looks like he just stepped out of a hamper. I can go on with grass stains.'"

The show hit big almost from the beginning, becoming the second most-watched show on MTV after *Beavis and Butt-Head*. The audience grew, and it also didn't hurt that guests loved doing the show. "Letterman's got a show he's doing, whereas this is much more casual," said Quentin Tarantino after appearing on both shows back-to-back. "This wasn't like doing a talk show. It was like we were just bullshitting."

"Usually, it's not fun doing publicity for a movie or show, but I genuinely enjoyed doing his show," said Daniel Baldwin, one of the Baldwin brothers, who was touting his role on *Homicide: Life on the Street* at the time. "He's quirky, he's nonchalant, and he lets you let your hair down. I would do his show again in a minute. It was a lot of fun. I even watch it now, and I never watch MTV."

Despite the pressure of essentially driving blind during his debut, there was less to lose on MTV compared with one of the major networks. "It was much easier to debut on a cable talk show," said Stewart. "There was no hype. It's much better when viewers find you as opposed to being told to watch you."

After six weeks of programs, he proved Stern wrong. MTV renewed the show and ordered another twenty-four shows. The *New York Post* called him one of the "hot new artists of the 90s."

The boy from Jersey was finally on his way.

The first season of *The Jon Stewart Show* was so successful that Viacom—which owned MTV—decided to capitalize on Stewart's popularity and move it to Paramount, a corporate division that handled syndicated TV shows, to fill an hour-long hole left in the wake of the cancellation of *The Arsenio Hall Show*.

While MTV was indeed a national cable channel, the size of its audience paled next to the programs that Paramount syndicated on the local affiliates of the major networks nationwide. In other words, the size of Stewart's potential audience was just about to get a lot bigger.

Stewart was thrilled. Not only would his show be syndicated across the country—not just aired on a niche cable channel—but it would be expanded from a half-hour to a full hour starting in September 1994.

He was also wary because the long show would require much more of his time and energy, and he had mixed feelings about that even after signing a five-year contract with Paramount. "I kind of liked my life [before]," he admitted. "I was enjoying myself on MTV. I was starting to branch out. I wouldn't have taken the gig unless I thought I'd be OK if I lost it. But if you're going to play it safe, don't be in show business."

His exhilaration didn't take long to wear off. The ratings soon began to tank, largely in part because under Paramount, he had to kowtow to higher-ups in charge of massaging syndicated content to appeal to a broad range of affiliate stations in markets all over America. Previously, at MTV, catering to slackers who were too lazy to change the channel after *Beavis and Butt-Head* ended had been his primary worry.

At one point, Paramount suggested that he wear a tie on the set. His response: "I guess it would be nice, if someone was getting married on the show.

"It seems a conceit that if you have your own show, you wear a tie," he said. "We do our show more from the hamper. Whatever we find that day floating on top that doesn't seem dirty—boom. It's right out there."

Comedian Lizz Winstead, Stewart's friend from the stand-up circuit, was asked to join the staff as talent coordinator. Her job was to find unknown but entertaining guests for the show, and she regularly combed through public-access cable TV shows for possibilities, but admitted it was a real challenge. "Some people are just crazy," she said. "You can't have them on because they're certifiable. There's this woman who thinks she's Underdog's girlfriend."

He also served as executive producer of the new version of the show, and he regularly skirmished with those from the executive suite. "When it comes down to content, *that's* where I choose my battles," he said. "If they say, well, we'd love it if you'd wear a black sweater tonight, I'll usually do that, but if they say, well we don't think that bit's funny, we don't want you to run it, I say, 'Well, we *do*,' so we put it on."

Also, filling one hour was a lot harder than just gabbing with minor and frequently unknown guests while occasionally punctuating a question by hurling a puck around the Nok Hockey table. Syndication also meant that individual stations decided when to air the show, and in some markets the only time they deemed to be available was three in the morning, which made it difficult to build an audience.

The stress and hours were beginning to take their toll. He was responsible for people, whereas with him doing stand-up, he only had himself to worry about. "The first four or five weeks, it was like every episode was *Broadcast News*. Ten seconds before it went on, somebody was sprinting down a hallway with the fat-guy tape," he said. But after the first month, he and the rest of the staff finally fell into a comfortable rhythm.

"We have to get comfortable with not running as fast as we

can," he said. "I think it'll help the show actually. There were a lot of times on MTV when I thought we gave our guests short shrift and now we won't have to. We just have to find the balance between short shrift and 'OK, that's enough, we get it.'

"A guy brought trained condors and one flew out in the audience, and we stood there dumbstruck while it bit an audience member's back," he said. "I was staring at this huge bird gawking in the audience while the trainer says, 'Hey, man, maybe you should go to commercial.' And I said, 'Hey, maybe you should get your bird.' The next night, Marilyn Manson was on and they ended up lighting the stage on fire. I really thought somebody was going to be killed that week."

Even though he and the staff adjusted, the audience in many cases didn't. "People did get used to our half-hour pacing, so when they watch it now, they think, 'Hey, this is supposed to be over! Make him stop!'" And even he had trouble with the hour-long format. "There are times when I'll just be sitting out there, thinking about my laundry.

"Trying to make a talk show compelling is the most difficult thing in the world," he said.

The pressure continued to build as the ratings dropped. What was worse was that in markets where the show aired in late-night prime time—at 11:30—he was up against not only Letterman, his hero, but also Jay Leno and *The Tonight Show*.

"Doing this gig is like when you see pictures of the presidents when they first get into office, and then two years later they look like shit," he said. "That's what's going to happen to me."

He also realized a surprising thing: with all of its hassles and risks, he actually missed performing live in front of an audience by himself. "One of the nice things about stand-up is you work on material" . . . and "give it time to breathe and live," he said. "When you're doing a monologue [on TV] every day, rather than discussing things that matter, it's, 'Hey . . . a guy fell into a vat of macaroni. [W]e can do something with that! . . . You start to lose sight of what you actually think."

Paramount pulled the plug and the last show aired on June 23, 1995. That day, Stewart and the production crew passed out margaritas to members of the audience and paid for their cab rides home.

"When it ended, I was blown out and exhausted, emotionally raw."

Stewart decided to take a few weeks off. However, unlike many New Yorkers in the entertainment business, he thoroughly disdained the chic summer getaway of the Hamptons. "The Hamptons are the most Hollywood place in New York, filled with all the people in New York you're trying to avoid," he said.

Instead, he retreated to his beloved Jersey shore. "You go down to the Jersey shore, lick your wounds for two weeks, and come back kicking," he said. "You can't just fold up the tents, you've got to refocus yourself and get back in it."

It was clear that doing the show had helped him to grow up, a lot. "When the show got canceled, I still knew how to write jokes the next day," he said. "That was a huge revelation.

Because at first you think, 'I won't have any shelter! What am I gonna do?'

"I shed a lot of the bullshit, the neuroses of earlier years. I still have my moments of abject panic, but I've been able to control it more as I've gotten older."

His mentor also gave him a few words of wisdom after the show ended. "Letterman said something that stayed with me: 'Never confuse cancellation with failure.'"

"As long as I don't end up hosting a skin care commercial with Cher, I'm happy," Stewart joked.

He returned to New York, refreshed and ready to make plans, when he was thrown for a loop: a month after the show was canceled, something even bigger happened than landing another show: he met the woman he'd end up marrying.

Though neither Stewart nor Tracey McShane, a veterinary assistant, had been on a blind date before, they arranged to meet at a Mexican restaurant after getting fixed up by one of Tracey's friends. And it almost didn't happen.

McShane had recently ended a long-term relationship and she didn't hold out much hope that she'd meet someone new, even though her friends were constantly playing matchmaker for her. Because her roommate worked in the entertainment business, she had been set up with a number of actors; unfortunately, the dates always bombed. Even though McShane had told her roommate, "No more performers," she had once mentioned that she would like to go out with someone like the host of a talk show that had just been canceled because she thought he was "funny and sweet."

With his schedule freed up, and because he was starting to entertain offers for acting jobs from Hollywood, he started to frequent movie sets in Manhattan, where he met McShane's roommate. One thing led to another, and the two arranged to meet. The initial reaction didn't go well.

They agreed to meet again, and within a few weeks they were inseparable.

CHAPTER 5

WITH HIS SCHEDULE changed from working seventy-hour weeks to zero, Stewart finally had a chance to think about what he really wanted to do. He decided to take his time figuring it out. He toured the country performing stand-up at the kinds of hole-in-the-wall comedy clubs that he had appeared at before he hit the big time. He also started to sift through the increasing number of offers that came in, ranging from movie deals to subbing for talk-show host Tom Snyder, who was at the helm of *The Late Late Show.*

Despite his new relationship with McShane, he decided to move to Los Angeles in order to develop these new opportunities, though he was understandably reluctant about leaving the New York area, where he had spent his entire life aside from college. He liked the fact that for the most part, New Yorkers didn't much care about celebrities.

"Everybody's got their own shit to worry about," he said. "I think that as long as I keep the music down, they're fine."

But sooner or later, Hollywood beckons many New York–based comedians and actors, and Stewart was no exception.

And when Snyder offered him the chance to occasionally substitute for him on his late-night show, Stewart decided to head west.

Snyder was a veteran talk-show host who had hosted *Tomorrow with Tom Snyder* from 1973 through 1982. With his background in hard news, the show had an inquisitive, thoughtful style, though his pointed questions were also interspersed with Snyder's opinions and comments; it was almost like watching two people hold court in a living room, punctuated with occasional sparring. Then, after more than a decade away from sitting behind a talk-show desk, Snyder had signed on to *The Late Late Show* in 1995, which was launched by David Letterman's production company Worldwide Pants as a way to hold on to viewers after his own show ended at 12:35 A.M. The irreverent Snyder was a great choice for that time slot and he would helm the show until the spring of 1999.

Stewart first sat in for Tom Snyder in the fall of 1996, and did so well that he became a regular substitute host, filling in every three or four months, usually for a week at a time. The difference in height between the two hosts—Snyder was six four to Stewart's five seven—provided for some memorable moments.

"The cameras [and furniture] were designed for his frame, so when I got there I looked like [Lily Tomlin's] Edith Ann character sitting in the chair," said Stewart. "They had to give me a booster cushion. So whenever I was working that show, I was actually sitting on a children's pillow."

And he sometimes acted like a kid, breaking into *The Price Is Right* studio with his friends after hours, where they took turns spinning the big wheel that served as the cornerstone of the game show.

Yet he felt like he could never totally relax and be himself while guest hosting. "When I was doing *The Late Late Show with Tom Snyder*, it was like house-sitting. So while it's nice, because it's a nice place to house-sit, you're still a little worried like, 'Oh my God, I just got ashes on the couch. Now what am I going to do?' You don't want to be the guy to fuck it up for when the other guy comes back and goes, 'Who drank all my whiskey?'"

Even though it was common knowledge that Snyder wouldn't stay on more than a few years because he wanted to retire, and some speculated that Stewart would make an ideal replacement, Stewart let it be known that it wasn't in the cards. He was hesitant to commit to another talk show so soon after the failure of *The Jon Stewart Show* at Paramount.

He took advantage of being in Los Angeles to branch out in his entertainment career. And just like after all the odd jobs he held after college, Stewart figured he might as well try everything. He hit the ground running, and then some.

He signed a deal with Miramax Films with his recently launched Busboy Productions company, which he named for one of the many part-time jobs he had held through the years. The pact committed Stewart to star in at least two film projects per year and offered him the chance to write and produce as well.

And even though he said he'd never do a syndicated show again, Stewart also signed a development deal with Letterman's Worldwide Pants company to eventually host and produce his own late-night talk show, one which would be totally on his terms where he wouldn't have to kowtow to a large entertainment company's executive brass.

It didn't take long before Stewart picked up small roles in popular TV shows like *The Nanny* and *NewsRadio*, and taped a couple of live stand-up performances that were later broadcast by HBO, including *Jon Stewart: Unleavened*. He also appeared in a number of small parts in movies where he appeared alongside some of the biggest stars of the time.

He thought his first big break would come in the 1996 movie *The First Wives Club* playing opposite Goldie Hawn, but his scenes ended up being deleted from the film. He followed that up with a role opposite Drew Barrymore in the romantic comedy *Wishful Thinking*, which also came out in 1996. The story was told by jumping between several different points of view— including Barrymore's and Jennifer Beals's, the other female lead—and turned mixed and missed signals into well-trodden jokes. Stewart played a nebbishy third or fourth wheel who in the end became Beals's love interest. To no one's surprise, least of all Stewart's, the film went straight to video.

Half Baked came next, where Stewart had a cameo role— billed as "Enhancement Smoker" in the end credits—of the cult stoner movie starring Dave Chappelle. The movie is about a group of pot-smoking friends who have to come up with the money to bail a buddy out of jail after he accidentally kills a diabetic police horse by feeding it junk food. Reviewers regarded it as the ultimate pothead film. Stewart followed up that role with another small part in *Since You've Been Gone*, a made-for-TV movie starring David Schwimmer about a disillusioned group of friends attending their tenth high school reunion.

Next up was the romantic comedy *Playing by Heart*—the original title was *Dancing about Architecture*—which featured a

Jon Stewart and Drew Barrymore at the premiere of *Wishful Thinking* in November 1995. *(Courtesy REX USA/ Rex)*

series of interlocking stories and a top-notch cast, including Sean Connery, Angelina Jolie, and Gillian Anderson. Here, Stewart's role was a bit meatier, as he played an architect named Trent intent on courting Anderson's man-shy character.

In all of his roles, Stewart's lack of acting chops was evident. It wasn't until he got the chance to play a different kind of role in the 1998 movie *The Faculty*, a flick about a group of high school students attempting to stave off an alien invasion, that it appeared he finally loosened up and looked like he was enjoying himself. Stewart played a biology teacher named Professor Edward Furlong who along with fellow actors Salma Hayek, Bebe Neuwirth, and Usher, of all people, is transformed into an alien after being infected with worms from space. One reviewer advised viewers to "Think of it as *Invasion of the Body*

Stewart and actress Gillian Anderson, his co-star, in a still from the 1998 movie *Playing by Heart. (Courtesy REX USA/Moviestore Collection/Rex)*

Snatchers enacted by the cast of *Scream*, an enjoyably dumb B movie."

Stewart's performance in all of these movies was unremarkable, a fact that he fully recognized. "The truth is, I'm not a good actor, but it's fun to try," he admitted.

"I trusted these people. I was hoping that they knew what I could do, and that was okay with them. I didn't go from being a talk-show host to being Sean Penn, I just went to being in a movie. I really felt like I didn't mess up, but I am really proud of it because I feel that I didn't mess up. I wasn't the burnt kernel in the popcorn. In that sense, I felt really proud of it that I held my own in this situation.

"[A]ll you can do is show up on the set, . . . and hope it works out. And then you go home and write your own stuff."

Some felt that Stewart's background as a stand-up comedian hurt his chances at succeeding in the movies. "While it's something that a lot of comics try to do, it's really hard to be able to play a role when people look at you and think of you as yourself," said Joey Bartolomeo, a senior writer at *US Weekly*. "If you look at someone like Jerry Seinfeld, his only role has been as Jerry Seinfeld on TV. You don't see him in movies playing other parts."

At the same time, Stewart credited his talk-show experience with helping his acting more than doing stand-up. "When you do stand-up, so often you're the only person on stage and it's all your thing," he said. "It's very gladiatorial. Obviously, when you're in a scene with somebody, you're supposed to listen and react—and that's a bit of a transition."

"As a stand-up comic, you don't work with other people," he noted. "As host, you're hanging on to every word people say because you have to react to it."

"It's nerve-racking to be with people who know how to act," he added. "Most comedians are doing themselves, ten percent angrier or happier. I like being able to do a little stand-up and do something else and also try acting. It's that neurotic vision: the more things that I can do, the more employable I'll be in the future."

While busy acting, he also started to miss doing stand-up. "I think comedians have this Pavlov's dog response when it comes to jokes," Stewart said. "You tell a joke, you get a laugh—and I miss the immediacy of that. With a movie or a book, you have hours of wringing your hands, wondering if people thought it was funny."

He was more of a natural in his occasional appearances on

Dr. Katz, Professional Therapist, an animated show that ran on Comedy Central from 1995 to 1999, but that was only because the show revolved around comics performing their routines while sitting on a psychiatrist's couch.

And then his most natural role appeared on the horizon in the form of *The Larry Sanders Show* on HBO, where he essentially played himself, a younger comedian who was being actively groomed and encouraged to replace an older mentor on a late-night talk show, played in the series by Garry Shandling.

Though he welcomed the steady gig, Stewart had misgivings about playing the role. "It's really one of the most uncomfortable places you can be," he said of his real-life predicament. "I think I realized I'd rather satirize who I am than be who I am."

Stewart appeared on several seasons of the show from 1996 through the last episode in 1998, and along the way as Shandling-as-Sanders spoke about leaving the fictitious show on some of the episodes, Stewart's character was rumored to step into the host's shoes on the show. Though Stewart played himself on the show, he acknowledged that the show's version of himself was rougher and ruder than how he presented himself on his own talk show on MTV and Paramount.

"But to play that character, I really couldn't play myself. I needed the protection of the character to do the awful things the character would need to do.

"At first, I was playing me, but not well," he said. "Then, in the last season, I got a full-blown story line and a chance to go outside myself. And to make it work, I really had to stretch."

Instead of just showing up for a segment or two for a few episodes each season, since the network executive characters on the show were trying to push Sanders out while grooming Stewart to succeed him, the real Stewart not only had to spend more time on the set but he also had more lines. Lines that required him to act rather than just crack jokes, which was what most of his movie roles had consisted of so far. For instance, once Sanders and his producer Artie—played by veteran actor Rip Torn—got wind of the executives' plans, several episodes revolved around the two backstabbing Stewart while they pretended that it was business as usual.

After his movie roles had gone nowhere Stewart started to sift through the deals he had made with both Miramax and Worldwide Pants. Though Miramax had broached the concept of a weekly sitcom, Stewart nixed it. "I was of the mind that, unless it was a great idea, I didn't want to do it," he said. "Just to do it for the sake of doing it wasn't a good idea. No one needs another halfhearted attempt."

With Letterman's company, talk turned again to a late-night talk show to come after *The Late Late Show with Tom Snyder.* But he was hesitant to try to replicate what he had done previously. He was thinking of writing a book, and just didn't want to tie himself down to another long-term television commitment. In the end both the Miramax and Worldwide Pants deals expired. Afterward, he went back on the road, on Comedy Central's nationwide Stand Up for Sanity tour.

Stewart had found that he liked pursuing several different projects at the same time rather than having one full-time gig. "Admittedly, at some point I'm probably going to have to settle down and sort of pick a discipline and stay with it for a little bit of time, but right now it's kind of nice to be able to float around and do a bunch of different things," he said.

As a result, one magazine writer called him "the celebrity equivalent of lint: he pops up in interesting and unlikely places."

There was also his growing discomfort in Los Angeles. A diehard New Yorker, he missed his girlfriend, Tracey. Their long-distance relationship had turned more serious. So he began to pull away from Hollywood with an eye toward returning to the East Coast.

The year 1998 would turn out to be a pivotal one for Stewart, and not just because he hosted a *Sesame Street* TV special called *Elmopalooza*, where he helped a variety of Muppets celebrate the thirtieth anniversary of *Sesame Street*.

For one, he was filming *Big Daddy*, a movie with hit potential that was shot in New York; it would hit theaters in June of 1999. When the project first came along, he didn't think much of the part, or the movie, for that matter. But it did give him a chance to work alongside his old stand-up buddy Adam Sandler, who had come up in the clubs of New York at the same time.

"I always used to try to borrow money from Adam when he was making fifteen bucks a night," said Stewart. "He was a soft touch."

Stewart played the role of Kevin Gerrity, roommate to Sandler's thirtysomething slacker Sonny Koufax. One day, Kevin surprises Sonny by dumping his five-year-old son at their apartment while Kevin flies to China for a business trip. Stewart turned the part from what could have been an extremely unsympathetic character into one with depth and wit.

"Jon had the trickiest part in the movie," said director Dennis Dugan. "He's in the first twelve minutes of the film and in that short amount of time, he has to make enough of an

Jon Stewart at the film premiere of *The Waterboy*, starring his *Big Daddy* co-star Adam Sandler, in New York, November 1998. *(Courtesy BEImages/ Matt Baron)*

impression . . . so that when he returns at the end, they'll go, 'I'm so happy that this guy came back!' And Jon achieved that."

Also in 1998, Stewart put the finishing touches on his first book. Though some expressed surprise at his desire to become an author, to him writing a book that consisted of a collection of comic essays was very similar to writing a series of inter-related stand-up routines.

"I get the sense that it's all the same thing, just in different forms," he said. "I don't look at it as that different."

Naked Pictures of Famous People would hit the *New York Times* best-seller list when it was published in September. But a month before that, Stewart received even bigger news:

He actually appeared first on a list to take over a talk show. Not second.

His old guest-hosting position on Tom Snyder's show was coming to an end: once Snyder announced his retirement, Letterman scouted around for a replacement. As usual, Stewart's name appeared on the short list, but in the end, Letterman chose Craig Kilborn for the job. Kilborn, who was then hosting a Comedy Central show called *The Daily Show*, accepted the position. Yet again, Stewart was second banana. However, with Kilborn's move the *Daily Show* spot had opened up.

"I always had my eye on [*The Daily Show*]," said Stewart. "But it's kind of funny, it's musical chairs. There are only five of these jobs available."

Kilborn had hosted the show since the launch of the half-hour program, designed to "report" on news of the day by giving it a satirical twist. He'd cut his teeth as a sports anchor, first at a Fox station in Monterey, California, and then as an anchor on ESPN's *SportsCenter*. Comedy Central had ordered *The Daily Show* into production to replace Bill Maher's show *Politically Incorrect*, which had switched networks to ABC.

When *The Daily Show* debuted on July 22, 1996, it was structured like any local newscast you could switch on anywhere in the country. Kilborn served as the news anchor, reading a few national news stories, which were followed by a few in-studio segments and field pieces from a correspondent or two. Since *The Daily Show* billed itself as a fake-news show from the beginning, the correspondents' stories followed suit. But the set's appearance fit the format.

"We just told the designers we wanted something that Ted Koppel would want for Christmas," said writer J. R. Havlan, who joined *The Daily Show* in 1996 when Kilborn started as host.

With Kilborn moving to take Snyder's job, there was an empty host's chair to fill at *The Daily Show*. Madeleine Smithberg, a producer who had worked alongside Jon on his previous show at Paramount, was now working at *The Daily Show*, and she thought Stewart would make a good host.

Stewart was under consideration—yet again—and he expected to come in second place as he had numerous times before. But he got one of the biggest surprises of his life when Comedy Central executives offered him the job. In addition to being *The Daily Show* host, he'd also share a co-executive producer credit. They struck a deal, signing him to a four-year contract paying him $1.5 million a year.

"There was only one name that came up," said Comedy Central president Doug Herzog. "We found the most talented free agent in the market."

"Jon will have a wider appeal to a greater age and gender," agreed Eileen Katz, senior vice president of programming at Comedy Central. "There's something that's more accessible about Jon as opposed to that whole *National Lampoon* school of comedians and hosts that looked very Ivy League and Midwest."

Many critics looked forward to his debut—and to getting rid of Kilborn. They—along with viewers—disdained Kilborn because of his almost constant smirk and frat-boy approach that infected the overall tone of the show and theme of many of the sketches. "He's certainly witty enough and articulate enough to host his own show, especially if he's replacing a guy like Craig Kilborn," said Adam Buckman, a TV columnist at the *New York Post*. "Jon's actually more talented at this sort of thing and can come up with funny things off the top of his head."

Stewart was ecstatic, and viewed the job as "sitting around with funny people, banging out jokes, and creating a television show. I have no hobbies, no outside interests," he said. "I'm fine with spending fourteen hours a day putting a show together with tape and string."

At the same time, he was realistic enough to know that his chances for longevity were not in his favor. "Whenever you take over something that is popular and has a fanatical following, you're never going to please everyone," he said. "The trick is to have enough wherewithal to follow through with what you want to do with it and give it time to evolve."

For once, he had come in first. But he had his work cut out for him. There had been a definite tension on the set, specifically between Kilborn and co-creator Lizz Winstead. Even though Winstead had been heavily involved in the initial development of the concept of *The Daily Show*, she had not been involved in the final decision about the show's first host.

"I spent eight months developing and staffing a show and seeking a tone with producers and writers, but somebody else [hired Kilborn]," she said. "There were bound to be problems since I viewed the show as content-driven while he viewed it as host-driven."

Eighteen months after the debut of *The Daily Show*, things had only gotten worse. In a 1997 *Esquire* magazine interview Kilborn made a few negative comments about the women who worked at the show, even calling them "bitches." He also said that he knew Winstead would "do a Monica Lewinsky" on him. When the magazine came out, the network suspended Kilborn for one week. Winstead quit shortly afterward.

Even with Winstead gone, the atmosphere on the show remained toxic. Several reviewers thought both Kilborn and the correspondents were working overtime to be nasty. "The take-no-prisoners attitude of this headline-oriented, half-hour sarcasm-and-shtick program [is] a slick combination of *Saturday Night Live*'s Weekend Update segment, moronic frat-house interplay, political humor, and surrealistic nonsense," said one.

Kilborn could be shockingly mean on the show. In 1997 the sentence was handed down in the 1993 World Trade Center bombing, and on air, Kilborn said the Twin Towers were occupied with a surfeit of stockbrokers. "Officials speculate that if the bombing had gone according to plan it would have taken a quarter of a million lives—and ten or twenty souls," he added.

"In the world inhabited and delineated by *The Daily Show*, everyone is an idiot," a *New York Times* reviewer wrote. "It's like making fun of the people in line at Epcot: too easy, but darned satisfying when you're cranky. And the central characters seem to have no idea that they'll be savaged when the piece is edited."

Correspondent Stephen Colbert started working for the show in 1997 and tried hard to keep away from the tension, yet he had misgivings about the tone of the stories he was called to report on. "You wanted to take your soul off, put it on a wire hanger, and leave it in the closet before you got on the plane to do one of these pieces," he said. "We had deep, soul-searching discussions on flights out to do stories, saying, 'We don't want to club any baby seals, I don't want to hold this person down and kick him in the teeth comedically.' But sometimes it would happen, because you had to come back with something funny."

For the most part, he stayed out of the fray. "I was so new there that I was kept completely out of any sort of political machinations there," he said. Even so, what did he think of Kilborn?

"He was really good at reading the teleprompter," said Colbert.

Even though he was stepping into an established show with a staff who were used to doing things a certain way, Stewart had already made up his mind that he was going to break away from the format and shake things up a bit. First and foremost, he wanted to make a difference in his own way.

"I decided not to give a crap about what anybody else thought anymore [and to do] what I wanted to do, with like-minded people who'd bring passion, competence, and creativity to it."

The truth was that critics didn't expect much from his new gig. In fact, one even viewed *The Daily Show* position as a step down for Stewart. "He once seemed destined for more," said the reviewer.

To start, he was the antithesis of Kilborn, who had a vain streak a mile wide; in between segments, Kilborn would compulsively fix his hair and makeup. When asked if he'd do likewise, Stewart said absolutely not, cracking, "There are no mirrors.

"The tone will obviously be a lot more Yiddish," he said. "I think at some point, I'd love to have a little bit of diversity. But as I keep saying, there is a certain mind-set that won't develop until I get there."

With that said, Stewart's neurotic streak reared up when asked what he'd think if the show would succeed. "I'm doing everything I can to sabotage my career," he said. "It's a little thing called fear of success, but really, a regular talk show can become your life. For ten years, it's your life. That is what you are and what you do." At the same time, he welcomed the challenge. "[*The Daily Show*] is a different kind of hosting than I'm accustomed to, it's a little less free-form, but we'll find out what I can do well and start tailoring it to that."

When Kilborn left, two other *Daily Show* regulars decided to exit as well: correspondents Brian Unger and A. Whitney Brown. Since Stewart's style was more of a *mensch* than the nasty guy that Kilborn played, Stewart believed that his more-optimistic outlook would have a top-down effect, spreading to the writers. But at the same time, he didn't want to rule anything out. "Hopefully the only things off-limits are crummy jokes, but being a stand-up comedian, I know that's not always the case," he said. "You know it when you have to take a shower afterward."

Despite industry speculation that he took the *Daily Show* job so that he could continue to do the occasional Hollywood movie, that was not his motivation. For one, the contract expressly specified that he couldn't take on a non–*Daily Show* gig for the first year, but it was clear—between the long days of sitting around on a set to the fact that he didn't really like acting—he just wasn't cut out for making movies.

It was rumored that Kilborn wanted to take a few of the *Show*'s segments with him to *The Late Late Show*, including the "5 Questions" bit, where the host asked his five rapid-fire questions. However, because Kilborn had broken his contract with Comedy Central, the legal team was much less inclined to negotiate with him. And so "Headlines," "Back in Black," featuring longtime contributor Lewis Black, and "A Moment of Zen" all stayed with the show.

To Stewart, it didn't much matter. He wanted to develop his own segments.

"You wouldn't want to take over for Letterman and start doing 'Top Ten' lists either," he said. "My feeling is basically the show's identity is going to have to evolve once I get in there. I'd love to have a little bit of diversity. Not just celebrities, but newsmakers."

"The structure of the show is very sound, so it's really a question of finding different flourishes," he added. "For the first few months, I'm sure I'll be stumbling around like when you first work in a restaurant. I'll be looking for where the ketchup is."

CHAPTER 6

WHEN JON STEWART debuted as the new host of *The Daily Show* on January 11, 1999, the critics were pleased.

"Happily, it was no trial to watch," wrote one reviewer. "A welcome return."

"Comedy Central did not lose in this game of late-night musical chairs," said another. "Stewart is more likable and less self-satisfied than Kilborn, and the show's satire is smart enough to have real sting. Now if only *Daily* could expand to an hour and allow Stewart's celebrity interviews to run longer than four breathless minutes."

"Stewart can barely keep a straight face delivering the nasty punch lines, and the disparity between his mildly neurotic persona and the show's gleefully raunchy tone seems to add to all the irony," wrote another. "I often still hate myself for laughing, but with Stewart, I forgive myself more easily."

Once the opening credits ran, Stewart took a deep breath and looked into the camera before announcing, "Welcome to *The Daily Show*. Craig Kilborn is on assignment in Kuala Lumpur, I'm Jon Stewart."

He then launched into a rapid-fire mix of the old routines while giving hints of his new approach and desperately trying not to alienate loyal viewers of the Kilborn version, which more often than not, tended toward frat-boy-style humor and pranks.

He interviewed actor Michael J. Fox while wearing a suit—a definite step up from the jeans and sweatshirt ensemble that had served as his nightly wardrobe on his previous talk shows—and admitted that he was more than a little nervous. "Honestly, I feel like this is my bar mitzvah," he said to Fox. "I've never worn something like this, and I have a rash like you wouldn't believe."

After the interview, correspondent Stephen Colbert weighed in with a report on the impeachment trial of President Bill Clinton and fellow correspondent Beth Littleford interviewed four of the original munchkins from the *Wizard of Oz*. In all, Stewart's first appearance set the tone for how the show would proceed in the future, as well as how it would be radically different from the program during the Kilborn era.

But the timing put him right in the crosshairs; not only were people watching to see how Kilborn's successor would excel—or flunk out—but also there was an enormous amount of material he had to work with, much like the political cartoonists who love it when things in Washington go awry.

While cast and crew maintained that the change in tone and content would be gradual, the truth was that with such a huge change and attitude at the top, it took only days for the audience to notice. For one, since Stewart was clearly more interested in politics than Kilborn, the show started running more political stories the very first week.

While correspondent Stephen Colbert had long considered himself to be apolitical, he experienced a radical shift once Stewart took over. "[The show] switched from local news, summer kicker stories, and celebrity jokes, to more of a political point of view," he said. "Since Jon has a political point of view, he wanted us to have one, too. I've always been a news junkie but I never wrote political satire before *The Daily Show*," said Colbert. "I didn't enjoy political humor until I started working on it with Jon, and then I found that I had a stronger one than I had imagined."

Conversely, over time, Stewart would find that working day in and day out on the show actually made him *less* political. "The more time you spend with the political and the media process, the less political you become and the more viscerally upset you become at the inherent corruption," he disclosed.

Yet Stewart didn't hit people over the head with the political content, instead suggesting to producers and writers that they try to shape correspondents' stories so that they had more of a connection to the news; after all, from the start, *The Daily Show* was billed as a news show, albeit a fake one. One of the complaints that correspondents had when Kilborn served as host was that the dichotomy between the news stories and correspondent reports was pretty radical.

Stewart wholeheartedly agreed. "Twenty-four-hour news networks [are] where a lot of the satire lies. News holds itself to a higher plane . . . There's a real hypocrisy about what these people have become. To see Barbara Walters criticizing a celebrity story when that's what they've become . . . now it's all confrontational."

"I have a lot of hostility [toward] the news media," he added.

"I have more trouble with the commentary on Clinton's affair than Clinton's affair. The self-righteousness is embarrassing.

"The news now is like a children's soccer game. Whatever the main focus of the day is where they go; it's not about territory and positioning. When one kid has the ball, everyone runs over there. And then he kicks it and everyone goes over there."

Stewart was also starting to lose patience more often with the media than with politicians. "I'm less upset about politicians than the media. I feel like politicians, there is a certain, inherent—you know, the way I always explain it is, when you go to the zoo and a monkey throws its feces, it's a monkey. But when the zookeeper is standing right there, and he doesn't say bad monkey.

"Somebody's got to be the zookeeper," he continued.

Stewart was also not a big fan of the network newsmagazine shows like *Dateline* and *20/20*. "You watch those shows and you'd think we were falling apart: 'You won't believe what's in that cheeseburger!' 'Did you know that your airbag could decapitate you?'"

But another distinct shift had taken place once Stewart took over. Previously the idea of the show being a total satire was a no-brainer. After Stewart came on board and put his spin on things, often in a sly, subversive way, it wasn't unheard of for viewers to become confused and think they were watching an actual newscast. As Madeleine Smithberg put it, it was no longer "crystal clear that we were a parody of the news.

"You really believed that Craig was that guy behind the desk," she said. "He looked like everyone you've ever seen on TV. Jon Stewart has an unbelievable range of things that he's capable of doing, but he delivers headlines like a guy telling jokes. He's brilliant, but you don't really believe he's a news anchor."

And in that fashion, the line between fake news and real news became blurred. And the overhaul that Stewart performed on the show from day one clearly reflected his slightly embittered view not only toward life but toward the news as well. "[What's funny about the news is] not the news itself but how the news is delivered," he said. "The parody is our bombastic graphics and the news song, the correspondents and their interaction with me. By using the general structure of a news show, which we find inherently satirical, we've found a cheap way to get in twenty monologue-type jokes."

"Oddly enough," he added, "*The Daily Show* is one of the most responsible news organizations because we're not pretending to be news in the first place. Our one rule is, no faking."

Unlike traditional news media, *The Daily Show* wasn't in the business of going out and finding news; instead, producers and writers only had to have the talent to review a day's worth of news and then retell it to their audience while giving it their own unique spin.

"One of the joys of being fake news is we don't actually have to break news," said Stewart. "We can just react to something we found interesting the day before."

"The more we pretend we're a news show, the clearer our comedy becomes," added Smithberg.

There were other benefits as well: occasionally, the news itself made the writers' jobs much easier: "[Sometimes] you don't try to top it with a written joke, because just on its own it can be pretty ridiculous," said Ben Karlin.

For that reason, executive producer D. J. Javerbaum said no

one ever worried about running out of material or missing a scoop. "It's a reactive show," he said. "As long as we're given things to react to, we'll be fine."

Indeed, as viewers and critics began to regard the content of *The Daily News* as journalism, Stewart was quick to correct them, with a caveat that took an interesting twist:

"I don't think what we do is journalism," but rather "analysis because we don't do anything but make the connections," he explained.

It was obvious from the beginning that the role of a fake news anchor fit him better than it did Kilborn, who was more interested in sports than the news. "I'm a little bit too obsessed with the news," Stewart admitted. "I find the news easier to follow than narrative entertainment programs. But I find the news, for me, I watch it like a program. I can't wait to find out what's happening with my favorite characters, like, 'Oh, I'm so sorry they dropped Saddam Hussein from the show. Oh, they're bringing him back!'"

He also discovered that he had missed having a regular mouthpiece for his opinions. "I'd not had a regular TV gig in three years," he said, "and I realized when I was on *Sanders* that the ability to comment in sort of a timely fashion is terribly important to me. While I still comment on it, I usually do it in my living room, and you begin to think of yourself as perhaps that creepy, bitter guy who sits on his couch and says, 'Can you believe this!?'"

He also looked forward to doing a good chunk of the writing on the show, unlike Kilborn who was content to just sit at the anchor desk. "That's really my favorite thing," he said, "sitting in a room with funny people till somebody hits on just the right bit."

Stewart laid down the law the first time he hung out in the writers' room, not only eliminating almost all of Kilborn's sophomoric frat-boy humor and segments, but also about clarifying the mixed signals the show was sending. "Half the jokes were about Barbie as a bad role model for girls, and the other half were about how ugly the spokesmodel was," said the new host.

But for the first couple of months, despite the positive response from critics, Stewart thought he had made a horrible mistake in accepting the job. A month before the switchover, he walked into a meeting of writers and producers on the show that was clearly hostile.

"I did not realize that a lot of the people who worked there were assholes," he said. "I walk in the door into a room with the writers and producers, and the first thing they say is, 'This isn't some MTV bullshit.' And then I was told not to change the jokes or improvise." As soon as he left the meeting, he called his agent and told him to "get me the fuck out of this, these people are insane."

Indeed, within a few months, several writers who had been there since the beginning gave notice that they were leaving, though Stewart said that it took over two years before the naysayers on staff were totally gone. He was not surprised that they left, but at the same time, he wasn't terribly upset either. "I can't tell you how relieved I was when people started walking [because] I didn't have to fire them," he said.

He hired Ben Karlin, who had written for the satirical newspaper *The Onion*, and he started working closely with correspondent Stephen Colbert.

He made no bones about the fact that his overall aim was to convey the news through the filter of his worldview while never losing sight of the fact that first and foremost he wanted to make people laugh.

He also wanted to work to make the tone of the show a bit kinder and gentler. "It's fair to say that at times *The Daily Show* can be a little too mean," he said of the show before he joined. "I happen to have a huge soft spot for all the eccentrics out there in America, and I think at its best, the show celebrates them." At the same time, he wasn't above knocking someone off a pedestal if it meant it would generate a big laugh. "The show is what it is, and if sometimes that means going out there and tearing Carol Channing a new asshole, well, I don't have a problem with that.

"Reality has gotten so absurd, it's almost like you're making it up, but as a comedian, [I'm essentially] cheering for the disillusionment of society," he conceded. "I'm hoping for chaos that I can muck with. And I have the utmost confidence that the world will provide it. I'm not hoping for the apes and the monolith, but that makes my job easier."

"Every day the world deals us a hand," Smithberg agreed. "And we've built a machine that can cope with it."

At the same time, Stewart and the crew were totally open to reinventing themselves along the way, to toss out what didn't work and to pounce on those segments that did. "This is a different kind of hosting than I'm accustomed to. It's a little less free-form. But we'll find out what I can do well and start tailoring it to that . . . It's less driven by me than the Paramount show was, but it will be ultimately driven by a certain comedic point of view that's different."

Because his previous talk show had been canceled he was pretty laid-back about the prospects for the show's failure, as well as his. But he was also pretty good at hiding the stress he felt. He had been a heavy smoker since his stand-up days, a habit he still clung to tenaciously. He liked to drink Coke from the bottle, and when the first one of the day had been emptied, he used it as an ashtray. When asked how many cigarette butts were in the bottle by the time he went home at night, he replied that he didn't know, "and counting would take all the fun out of it."

But by all outward appearances, Stewart seemed pretty relaxed. "For me, a talk show was never really the goal," he said. "People that worry about where they're going next generally don't end up where they think they're going. I just worry about what I'm doing now and try to make it good. When you've got too much of a master plan, it's going to fail."

Once Stewart had settled into his job and the staffers became comfortable with their new direction, it was time to hire a couple of new correspondents since Brown and Unger, who'd left when Kilborn departed, hadn't been immediately replaced. Producers wanted to be sure to match any new correspondents with the new direction of the show. They asked around the studio for suggestions, and Colbert suggested Steve Carell, who he'd worked with at Second City and on *The Dana Carvey Show*.

In the meantime, Stewart had begun to transform the job of fake anchor—which Craig Kilborn had always delivered with a healthy dose of smugness—into something uniquely his own. Instead of conveying fake headlines with a huge wink to the audience as Kilborn had done, Stewart's tone took on more of an inclusive air, more of a sense of being in on the joke, as if he were saying, "Can you believe these guys?"

Even though the show was now *The Daily Show with Jon Stewart*, whereas Craig Kilborn's name hadn't appeared anywhere in the show's title, one thing that viewers found refreshing about the show was that even though Stewart set the tone of the show, it wasn't about him, but about his ability to share the absurdity of current events with an audience of people who could definitely appreciate it. "Jon Stewart has brought back a kind of an everyman intellectualism," said Brian Farnham, then editor-in-chief of *Time Out New York*. "He was that smart guy you knew in college [who] was funny and saying the thing that you were thinking and wish[ing] you could say."

Stewart concurred.

The show was a natural fit for him, he was enjoying himself despite the breakneck schedule of cranking out four shows each week, and the job clearly was not going to go away anytime soon. As a result, Jon appeared to, well, become more *Jon*. "I always liked him, but when he became Jon Stewart he seemed to become more content with who he was," said Noam Dworman, who owned the Comedy Cellar where Stewart had cut his teeth in stand-up. "He seemed to be where he was and felt he should be, and it seemed to have a relaxing effect on his personality."

Even though he became more *Jon* on *The Daily Show*, Stewart said that just like his stand-up persona was a more exaggerated version of himself, the same applied to his TV host persona.

"It's pretty close, but also not close in the sense of I don't live my life like it's a half hour, like it's a show, it's a performance," he said. "At home, I don't go to commercial after breakfast. I'm not playing a character, it's just a heightened performance."

He did admit that after years of starts and stops, *The Daily Show* was where he hit on all cylinders. "The only things that I am able to do, I am able to do here," he said.

For maybe the first time in his life, he was being true to himself.

"I think people are responsible for themselves, for the most part," he added. "I think you're responsible to present yourself, to be as positive a person as you can be, whether it's because you're Jewish or black or Asian or whatever you are. I honestly think we'd be so much better off if that's what people focus on. There's really one rule: the golden rule. Focus on that, and it really doesn't matter."

Lest some people think he was solely on the lookout for a news hook or story to turn into a joke, the daily headlines of that first year on the air were not all fair game for Stewart and the team. "All of the images coming out of Kosovo were so horrific, you think, . . . 'There's nothing funny about this,'" he said. "And then . . . 'Fabio got hit in the face with a goose!' . . . It was like receiving a gift from the gods."

Part of the reason why Stewart seemed more settled was simply because in addition to his professional life becoming more established, the same thing was happening in his personal life. He and his girlfriend, Tracey, were now living together in a loft in downtown Manhattan, and they were engaged to be married.

One of the things that won her heart from the beginning was when they played games together.

He had proposed in a unique way: he asked Will Shortz, the crossword editor of the *New York Times*, for help. They had met previously when they were both guests on *Late Night with Conan O'Brien* and became friends. A few months later, Stewart asked Shortz if he could drop a few hints into an upcoming crossword puzzle since both he and Tracey loved to work on the puzzle each day.

"It was two days before Valentine's Day and Jon comes home and says, 'I remembered to bring those crossword puzzles home,'" said Tracey. "As I start to fill it out, there are all these words in it that relate to us."

"There were [a few] little things in there that related to her," he said.

One of the hints was "1969 Miracle Met baseball player Art." The answer, Shamsky, also referred to their dog named Shamsky, who Stewart referred to as his best friend. Shamsky was a rescued pit bull who Stewart claimed was agoraphobic and needed much coaxing to go outside.

"They're very misunderstood animals," he said. "At the pound in New York, they're pretty much the most common animal, I'm sorry to say. People think of them as vicious soldiers, but they're actually quite sweet and playful. People get them for certain purposes that they don't work out for and then they discard them. Shamsky unfortunately was not treated particularly well early in life, so I think she has some residual emotional damage. Although you could say that probably about most people you meet."

Another hint in the puzzle was "tool company," which pertained to their cat named Stanley. "Then another clue was 'Val-

Stewart works diligently on one of his favorite pastimes—the *New York Times* daily crossword puzzle—in *Wordplay*, a documentary about the newspaper's puzzle editor Will Shortz. *(Courtesy REX USA/c.IFC Films/Everett)*

entine's Day Request,' and it's 'Will you marry me?'" said Tracey. "[The next] clue was 'Recipient of the Request.' I look at it saying, 'It almost looks like my name could fit in there.'"

It did. They were married in 2000.

He was so grateful for his newly happy, settled life that he finally buckled down under Tracey's pressure and quit smoking cold turkey that same year. "I didn't realize it at the time, but after you cut out smoking, drinking, and drugs, you feel much better," he said.

He was profoundly grateful for finding Tracey. "Let me put it this way, I know that I married up," he said. "And I know how women felt about me before television. When I was a bachelor, I did fine, but usually it had to do with the fact that I was bartending or had a show."

As they prepared to start a family, they filed a motion with the court to change both of their names to Stewart; legally, Jon was still known as Leibowitz, and some speculated that he made the change in order to put one more step between him and his still estranged father, especially since he was eagerly looking forward to becoming a father himself.

But they weren't certain if that would come to pass. They tried several rounds of in vitro fertilization treatments and tried hard not to become discouraged and anxious.

Stewart was also making his peace with religion, a concept that had dogged him since he was young. "Religion was one of the things I was hung up on in childhood that I sort of worked out," he said. "It always baffled me. I tend to need logic in my life; I'm very poor with faith. While I do believe in God, I just don't think he's still looking out for us. I mean, if you think about it, he created the world in six days—five billion years ago! Don't you think by now he's moved on to another project? Maybe we're just something he threw together for his third-grade science fair in the first place."

"I don't have a problem with religion," Stewart once explained to Larry King. "I think that religion provides a lot of people with comfort and solace, but you know, I think what people who aren't that religious object to is [the belief] that the only way to find values is through religion."

And though others wondered about his mixed marriage—Tracey was raised Catholic—Stewart joked about the situation as usual. "My wife is Catholic, I'm Jewish, it's very interesting: we're raising the children to be sad."

. . .

Happily, viewership of *The Daily Show* grew. Ratings increased steadily from the first night that Stewart held court. The critics weighed in:

"I think the reason why people watch *The Daily Show* is because they have found, first of all, that it is extraordinarily funny," said Devin Gordon of *Newsweek*. "They have found a place that is both extraordinarily funny and doesn't insult their intelligence, which is a rare combination nowadays."

Said David Hinckley, critic-at-large at the New York *Daily News*, "It actually serves a legitimate news purpose in my night. It is another reinforcement of what people are talking about because it has a pretty good pulse for what's on people's minds."

Bob Schieffer, host of *Face the Nation* on CBS, had this to say: "Jon Stewart is to television what the editorial page cartoonist is to the editorial page of newspapers. The editorial page cartoonist is the only person at the newspaper who is allowed to lie. I see Stewart as an editorial page cartoonist. A lot of time, by taking something beyond where it is, it helps you to drive home a point and really understand the truth."

Indeed, compared with the other late-night shows, *The Daily Show* was different not only in tone but in format. "Basically, Letterman and Leno have to get through those ten-minute opening monologues [while] the fuel of their shows is often more guest-driven," said Stewart. "[By contrast], we had to fill our half-hour every night with something. Not that those four minutes with [guests like] Tiffani-Amber Thiessen aren't enjoyable. Don't get me wrong, she tells a hell of a story. But I think we would go insane if we had to spend our whole day trying to think of synonyms for dumb, if we hadn't looked for larger arcs in the comedy."

Another reason why he and the producers decided to keep a guest segment in each show was for sheer utility: it absolved the writing staff from having to develop another five or six minutes of jokes and routines.

Though Stewart had his own ideas as to why people reacted so strongly to the show, in the end, every monologue, sketch, and interview came down to what he cared about most and how he wanted to convey that to his audience. "I think for me in some respects I am attempting to scratch an itch," he said. "And I want to make humor about things I care about. And unfortunately, the larger issues are probably more deeply affecting to me than most things."

CHAPTER 7

THE WHOLE TONE of the show had shifted in the year since Stewart came on board as host. Whereas previously, stories about Bigfoot and taxidermied squirrels would have automatically been green-lighted, now the future of such pieces was uncertain. "As soon as the presidential campaign started up in 2000, you could see the show begin to change," said Colbert. In fact, at the end of the 2000 campaign season, Colbert—newly politicized—offered up a bet to the other correspondents and producers. "I put a hundred dollars on the table and said to the field producers, if you can get us a Bigfoot story, I'll give you the hundred-dollar bill," he said. "I knew none of that shit was going to get past Jon anymore. Everything had to be grounded in reality, in something that's happening in the world, so we could use our field pieces as an addition to the satirical take that's happening at the desk."

"Some of the correspondents on *The Daily Show* write more than others, some are more traditional performers, but in almost all cases input is pretty welcome," said Karlin, "anything that can help make it in their own voice. Colbert is the most experienced writer, so he writes or rewrites a lot of his own stuff."

With the first year of *The Daily Show with Jon Stewart* under his belt—and very positively received—in early 2000 Stewart felt he could finally bring out the big guns and turn more of the focus of the show to politics. Then again, with the upcoming 2000 presidential election, he had little choice. And given the tone of his commentary and stories in the first year, Stewart's own political leanings were no secret.

"I've always felt [that] what is defined as leftist [is] relatively reasonable," he said.

"I have a tendency to lean toward the underdog, which I assume is the liberal perspective," he acknowledged, "but as I've gotten older, I find I've developed my own ideology. I don't really fit into anything."

"In the beginning of 2000, the content became far more political," said writer J. R. Havlan. "When the election came up, we were in a unique position, and Jon realized this is what we're here for. That's when we started to focus on media coverage."

Just as Stewart's visibility and reputation were starting to achieve critical velocity, the 2000 presidential election cycle began. Certainly there was no better place to exercise his muscles and to make a statement than at the party conventions in 2000. "We are definitely a fake news show, and political conventions are definitely a fake news event," he said. "So, in some respects, we're probably the only news organization who should be here."

In fact, choosing to call the *Show*'s coverage of the 2000 campaign and election season Indecision 2000 was a brilliant stroke of genius that at once sent a message of what viewers could expect as well as mock the stance of more conventional news media. However, when they first came up with the moniker, no one on the staff of *The Daily Show*, least of all Stewart, had any idea how prescient that term would turn out to be, as the results for the November 7 elections were still not determined even after a month of a contentious round of recounts was conducted in Florida, which had been too close to call, and until the U.S. Supreme Court stepped into the fray and basically called the race for George W. Bush.

But viewers were noticing how Stewart's election coverage was radically different from the shows their parents watched. In fact, for *The Daily Show*'s Indecision 2000 election night special, almost as many younger viewers tuned into Comedy Central as those who were watching the results come in over at Fox News. *The Daily Show* measured 435,000 viewers aged 18 to 34 compared to 459,000 in the same category at Fox. Since Stewart took over as anchor the previous year, *The Daily Show* averaged two million viewers a night, which was huge for cable and significantly higher than Kilborn's numbers, which typically hovered around one million.

Though Stewart scorned both parties in almost equal doses, he held special rancor for how the media reported the campaign and its aftermath, failing to hide his disgust. "This isn't Olympics boxing, it's a presidential race," he said. "[The media] set up expectations in that first debate as, literally, if George Bush proved he could feed himself, that was presidential, and if Al Gore blinked, he had warmth. And that's the way they judged the debate. They didn't even deal with the fact that when an issue did come up, George Bush's proposals were literally, 'I think Americans are good. And should help themselves.'"

The uncertain outcome of the election fanned the flames

of *The Daily Show*, attracting thousands of new viewers to the show since it could rightfully be argued that the hanging chads and circus-like atmosphere of conventional news reports helped not only to develop Stewart's chops but also to build a loyal audience that would stick around long after the winning candidate had settled into the Oval Office.

"Everything [in the campaign] became so absurd that the absurd people became the actual pundits," Smithberg said. "Jon Stewart is now a kind of recognized, viable pundit."

"There was no better story for us than the 2000 election because it involved everyone, it was unprecedented, and no one died," said Colbert. "The night that Gore conceded, we were finally able to use the material we were writing for thirty-two days. It was so much fun to release all that comedy that had built up for that time. I couldn't imagine having more fun. We all felt that way."

More important, the *Show*'s coverage of the convention helped put both the show and Stewart on the map. "[I]n the year 2000 Jon Stewart officially became a public intellectual," said Robert Thompson, director of the Bleier Center for Television and Popular Culture at Syracuse University.

"We've always wanted to be less dependent on the Hollywood cycle of standard talk-show guests," said Ben Karlin. Though it had been tough to convince name-brand guests to come on the show for a couple of years, it finally turned around. Again, Karlin credited the campaign season. "The show made a name for itself during the elections as a place where politicians or journalists would want to come and talk."

For his part, Stewart mixed his opinions with a caustic humor, and had this suggestion for future election seasons: "I think what we should do at five P.M. on election night is all walk outside and raise our hands for one of the two candidates and just have a helicopter fly over," he said. "I just think it would be easier. The idea that some people vote on machines and other people pick a bamboo stick that's shorter than another, the whole thing is ridiculous."

The hard work and notice were recognized the next year when the show won a prestigious Peabody Award, given to broadcast outlets to recognize the best programs of the year. Other winners that year included *The West Wing* and *The Sopranos* and single episodes of *48 Hours* and *Dateline NBC*.

Everyone who worked on the *Show* improved their game even more, spurred on not only by the national recognition but also by witnessing their boss's work ethic. "I was shocked at how much thought and distillation he personally puts into the script," said Colbert. "His care and unbelievable work ethic, and ability to consume information, digest, and distill a story. He's telling us that this is the mechanics of the human interaction, and this is the actual message of the story." Colbert, perhaps more than the other correspondents, took to heart Stewart's palpable disdain for the traditional news media and used it to help shape his own character. "He's naming what seems most ridiculous about the news, which is the personalities and the news itself," Colbert said. "It's only the overt game that's being reported."

During the 2000 campaign season, while *The Daily Show* began to gain critical mass among viewers, traditional media began covering the show itself. During the days leading up to the election, news shows on the networks—like the *Today* show—were running brief segments from the previous night's episode on a regular basis. "It's like they've handed over the reins of commentary and reporting to comedians because we're the only ones who can make sense of it," said Madeleine Smithberg. She and other staffers had mixed feelings about their newfound standing. "Our currency is one of insanity. Stop giving us credibility! We don't know what to do with it, it's messing up our shtick."

What happened next was entirely predictable, if not a bit uncomfortable: the major news programs and networks started to invite Stewart onto their programs to boost ratings and appeal to a younger demographic than usual. His reluctance to make the rounds was not just due to the early hour.

"It's weird to be anywhere at seven thirty A.M., that's when I should be fast asleep with my dog," he said. But there was another, more important issue. He felt that when he was interviewed by traditional media people—particularly on TV—that while they didn't strictly treat him as a comedian, they didn't quite take him seriously either. "The difference between myself and the analysts on a show like *Today* is when I'm introduced, they either say, 'Now for a look at the lighter side of politics,' or, 'Comedians have been making hay with this election, for that take . . .' It's never Gore's speech that sets up my segment, it's Jay Leno's joke."

In a sense, Stewart wanted it both ways: though he always maintained he was a comic first and not a newsman, he took issue with his treatment on the major news networks and programs, when they did regard him as "just" a comedian.

After all, in the two years between the first time he hosted *The Daily Show* and the show where they announced that George W. Bush would be the new president, Stewart had come a long way. And since he didn't even try to hide his disdain whenever he appeared on a network news show, in many instances his appearances combined light chitchat with a bit of finger pointing followed by the inevitable and uncomfortable silence from his on-air hosts.

But perhaps the thing that got him incensed the most was when his on-camera interviewers disclosed to him off-camera that they envied him. "The thing that shocked me the most was when I first met reporters who would tell me, 'Boy, I wish I could say what you're saying.' You have a show! You're a network anchor! Whaddya mean you can't say it?" he said. "It's one reason I admire Fox. They're great broadcasters. Everything is pointed, purposeful. You follow story lines, you fall in love with characters: 'Oh, that's the woman who's very afraid of Black Panthers! I can't wait to see what happens next.'"

The next statement might surprise his fans. "Fox News and our show have a tremendous amount in common," he said. "We are both reactions to the news and to government and . . . expressions of dissatisfaction."

Stewart made no secret of his disdain for CNN. "Their version of clarity seems to me to be like grits without salt. It's just all mashed up—there's no direction, under the guise of 'integrity.' I can never figure out what the hell I'm watching," he said. "With other networks, you either agree or disagree with how they do stuff, but CNN feels like an opportunity squandered."

However, some news stars were absolute fans, and Stewart didn't mind them as much. After CNN anchor Wolf Blitzer taped a segment for the show, Jon asked if he could hang out for a bit. Blitzer quickly agreed. "How could I say no?" he asked. "This is the most important show ever."

"There's no doubt he's an important fact of life in this current political environment," Blitzer said. "Off camera, he's a very politically aware news junkie."

In Stewart's eyes, his exchanges with TV interviewers seemed like a hall of mirrors. "On television, . . . operatives for both political parties will say, 'John Kerry's the most liberal' or 'The jobs created are nine thousand dollars less,' and nobody ever says, 'Where do you come up with these numbers?'"

This desire to press until he gets a clear answer came out loud and clear when former Republican congressman Henry Bonilla came on the show and Stewart asked him how his party came up with the formula where they declared that then-senator John Edwards was "the fourth most liberal senator." Bonilla didn't answer the question and the line between what Stewart does and what journalists do became further blurred when Stewart complained that most TV journalists don't question their guests like he does.

He didn't work to hide his contempt for politicians on the show, though he directed his producers and bookers to bring more of them onto the show. "If you feel like comedy program bits are your best effort as far as selling your candidate, good luck to you," he said.

"These people are salespeople," he added. "Instead of rotisserie ovens they are selling this idea of preemptive war or social-security reforms."

At the same time, he declared a basic tenet of the tone of *The Daily Show* that he'd repeat many times in his own defense. "We're not provocateurs, we're not activists; we are reacting for our own catharsis," he maintained. "There is a line into demagoguery, and we try very hard to express ourselves but not move into, 'So follow me! And I will lead you to the land of answers, my people!' You can fall in love with your own idea of common sense. Maybe the nice thing about being a comedian is never having a full belief in yourself to know the answer. So you can say all this stuff, but underneath, you're going, 'But of course, I'm fucking idiotic.' It's why we don't lead a lot of marches."

Of course, this was a completely fresh take on TV, whether it was his show or the more traditional news programs on cable or network, which underscored another reason the shows had for booking him: "These guys have twenty-four hours to fill," he said. "They've got to come up with something. If these guys did what they *should* be doing, forty-five minutes into their newscast they'd turn to the other guy, say, 'I'm out of here,' and then they'd leave."

But Stewart found it more difficult to hide his disgust at a new and rapidly growing trend in the news media: in the wake of the Gore vs. Bush debacle, some of these shows actively introduced a style of program that was most prominently on display on the CNN show *Crossfire*, which pitted two people with diametrically opposed viewpoints and let them go at it on live TV. Stewart hated this format because he felt the shows were based purely on opinion with little to do with real news value.

"It's the WWF," he said. "These shows are all about conflict. Whatever the situation is, they take a liberal pundit and a conservative pundit—the more extreme the better—and let them yell at each other. It doesn't reflect anyone's opinion. It doesn't matter."

If anything, his disgust with both sides was hard to hide, and actually turned the self-proclaimed liberal into a voice for the moderate middle, at least temporarily. "We're moderates!" he proclaimed. "Moderates never mobilize quickly. Moderation doesn't inspire passion. That's the thing about being a moderate. You're not the person standing outside the voting booths in Miami/Dade County to stop people from doing the recount. Moderates have a life. Or they're home cleaning the gutters or something."

Despite Stewart's contempt for much of the news media, it continued to flock to him, bestowing him with honors and awards and inviting him onto more shows and programs, as well as to host awards shows. He agreed to some offers, including the Grammy Awards in both 2001 and 2002.

He was obviously thrilled when *The Daily Show* won accolades from establishments he actually respected. *The Daily Show* won an Emmy for Outstanding Writing for a Variety, Music or Comedy Program in 2001, and Jon felt that somebody out there finally respected him. In addition to winning the same Emmy for writing for the majority of the next decade, *The Daily Show* would also proceed to win an Emmy for Outstanding Variety, Music or Comedy Series each year for the next decade starting in 2003, an unprecedented feat.

And then, the old world started to knock on his door again. Just as Stewart's four-year contract with Comedy Central was coming up for renewal in 2003, David Letterman started to float rumors that he was thinking of moving his show to ABC when his own contract expired. As before, Stewart's name was considered as a possible replacement, but now with his own star in ascendance and so many people clamoring for a piece of him, there was little chance that he would ever come in second place again. In the end, Letterman stayed put at CBS, but intriguingly, ABC upped the ante and offered Stewart his own late-night show to shape as he wished.

As he pondered the offer, however, the network pulled a fast one and instead took the offer to Jimmy Kimmel, who pounced on it. At the time, Kimmel had just launched his own talk show on ABC, *Jimmy Kimmel Live!*, after serving as cohost of *Win Ben Stein's Money* and *The Man Show*, which aired on Comedy Central in the late 1990s.

Amazingly, despite the accolades and his now iconic status, Stewart still came in second. However, this time he didn't seem to mind. The truth was that as his star continued to rise, Stewart retreated further inward whenever he was away from the studio. He was gracious with fans whenever approached, offering up an autograph and sometimes a joke, but otherwise he went into deep retreat whenever he wasn't at the studio. Indeed, one reporter called him "a high-functioning hermit."

In the early 2000s when it seemed the rest of the country was attached to their computers and the era of smartphone ubiquity was just around the corner, Stewart still didn't have an e-mail address, at home or at the studio. "Don't you find that people contact you way more?" he responded when someone asked the reason why. Indeed, he is rarely seen on the Manhattan celebrity circuit, only emerging to make the obligatory appearance at the annual awards shows where he's been nominated. Stewart is a content homebody, and once he found a kindred spirit in Tracey—whom he married in 2000—he had little reason to stray from his favorite activities away from work: doing the daily *Times* crossword puzzle, watching TV, and taking the dogs—he had added another pit bull named Monkey to the household—to the park.

"I was a fan of *The Little Rascals* and Petey was a pit, so maybe that was inherent," said Stewart. "If you go to the store and buy the generic 'dog,' that's the dog. That little block head and that little dog body, and so energetic and playful. They're meaty and muscular and fun."

And then an interesting thing began to happen. Word on the street and at many college campuses was that many young people who never watched network news were watching *The Daily Show* regularly and considering it their primary source of news, particularly when it came to the 2004 presidential election season.

"I'm not watching the evening news to figure it out, that's for sure," Joe Harper, a twenty-one-year-old college student, commented in early 2004. Instead, he relied on Dennis Miller, Bill Maher, and *The Daily Show* to get his information. "I trust these guys," he added. "Their stuff is funnier, but it's also truer."

Harper was in good company. A 2004 survey released by the Pew Research Center revealed that fully one-fifth of Americans aged 18 to 29 said they relied on not only *The Daily Show* for their main source of news about the presidential candidates but *Saturday Night Live* as well.

Comedian Miller weighed in. "I don't think kids even vaguely connect to guys like [Peter] Jennings and Dan Rather," he said. "If you're an eighteen-year-old, who are you going to trust to give you the facts? Dan Rather in that epaulet jacket where he's just about to go fly-fishing after the show, or are you going to listen to Jon Stewart? Of course, you're going to listen to Jon."

"It sounds a little bit apocryphal to me, but we do repackage the news, so I suppose that we are a valid source as long as people can understand when we're goofing and when we mean it," said Colbert. "I think you have to have some handle on what's happening in the world to get our jokes, because we only do the most cursory explanation of what the issue is in order to set up our punch lines. We don't talk in depth about any stories. I suppose you could watch our show and sort of get a sense of what's going on in the world, but you'd also be missing half of our jokes."

"I find it hard to believe," said Stewart. "I enjoy the show as much as the next guy, but we don't actually give any news. If you haven't seen the news, you probably won't know much about what we're talking about. We're a cable channel. I mean, we're beyond Spanish people playing soccer on the dial, we're near a naked talk show. My guess is if you found your way to us, you're a relatively savvy consumer of information."

"Different outlets have been saying that for a while or claiming studies [demonstrate] the show's influence on the public," said writer J. R. Havlan. "We don't sit around thinking about it. We don't come in and say, 'How are we going to affect the media landscape? Are we going to increase the number of kids who get their news from *The Daily Show*?' There's no insidious plan."

If anything, the show teaches viewers to think and dissect the news that's presented to them, regardless of the medium. "The show provides people a lesson in skepticism," said Havlan. "That's the biggest service. I mean, we're not even interpreting things, I think it's more truthful than that. Network news—not just cable—has to be constantly questioned, and our show is uniquely positioned to do that."

For his part, Stewart discounted the studies and surveys. "I'd be awfully surprised given the magnitude of media available," he said. "Younger people are far more inundated with information than we ever were. We're suffocating in information."

And when it came to deciding which stories to cover—after all, with a twenty-four-hour news cycle, there are always plenty of stories out there that just beg to be satirized—there are additional issues to tackle, among them responsibility to the story and the culture. "We try to cover stories that are interesting to people and, more importantly, relevant," said Karlin. "I think we'd be a lot more into finding something that's inherently funny and quirky, but then we['d] have to educate the audience a lot more. Instead, we'd rather talk about what's on people's minds or what's particularly absurd of this moment or of this time.

"We try not to measure the reaction to the show as much as our own internal barometer," he added. "I don't want to take the temperature of how people are receiving it, because I think that would affect how we're producing it. When we see something we find absurd or interesting, we try and write jokes about it or come up with something interesting to say about it."

As the ratings continued to climb, politicians began to notice that an appearance on the show could boost their visibility with a younger demographic virtually overnight. Though some might shudder at the idea of being interviewed or featured in a story on *The Daily Show*, others embraced the opportunity.

"Politicians love him and they respect him because he is a very intelligent guy," said Neil Rosen, entertainment critic at the *New York Times*. "But I also think they do the show because they understand that it is a very smart audience that is watching. They are also an audience who votes. And as soon as you walk onto that set as a politician you have adopted [Stewart's] credibility."

However, that comes with a caveat: for the most part, the politicians who flocked to the guest chair opposite Stewart were Democratic. Republicans started to complain, but Stewart maintained that he never hesitated to lash out at hypocrisy in the Democratic Party when the opportunity presented itself. He also thought that politicians made for more sparkling conversation than actors, musicians, or authors in many cases.

"I just think politicians are more interesting to talk to," he said. "Not that I'm not fascinated with the exact date a movie is coming out, but in general, I think it's slightly more interesting probably to talk to somebody who does something completely different from what I do."

At the same time, given the tone of the show as well as the format, if they weren't promoting a book or movie the majority of people who agreed to go on the show did so to make a specific point. "People don't typically come on our show unless they're disgruntled," Stewart said. "Then they come on the show to express their disgruntlement. We are the last stop of the disgruntled."

For this reason, they also made easy targets, though Stewart maintained that he always tried to resist the lazy joke. "The show is not a megaphone," he said. "You can't end every joke with 'Let's bomb the motherfuckers,' even though that's how I feel. But I take some pleasure in just ridiculing al Qaeda. When we got the Kandahar tape"—the video released in December 2001 in which Osama bin Laden confessed to being the mastermind of the September 11 terrorist attacks— "our first instinct was to . . . lay down fart noises, . . . because he hates to be laughed at."

Little was sacred when considered for their crosshairs, and even Comedy Central basically left the show alone. One of Viacom's top brass actually referred to the show as "the latchkey kid." One of the few hard-and-fast rules they ran into was that "dildo" couldn't be mentioned in a show four times; but three was okay.

"Humor is such a subjectively weird genre," Stewart said. "One man's meat is another man's poison, it's so hard to say this is what's allowed, but this isn't. So we vacillate. Some days our heels are planted firmly in the ground and we're ready to fight, and other days we're washing our hands thirty times because we think we have anthrax."

All the while he was determined not to cater to the lowest common denominator. It just wasn't his way. "There's a certain school of comedy that mistakes edge for the obnoxious. I find that the best comedy, the most edgy stuff, is rooted in a way of thinking about something that other people haven't come to yet. To me, that's edgy."

Surprisingly, advertisers didn't mind when they fell victim to Stewart's criticism. "If the show is going to go after an advertiser, we call the advertiser with a heads-up, but we tell him, 'If Jon is making fun of you, it's a plus,'" said Larry Divney, president of Comedy Central in 2002. "It means you're being talked about!"

Besides, the exposure could be worth it. Three years after Stewart took the helm, seven hundred thousand people were watching the show each night; Kilborn had barely half the viewership. In January 2005, *The Late Late Show with Craig Kilborn* morphed into *The Late Late Show with Craig Ferguson* after Kilborn decided not to renew his contract and left the program.

For his part, Stewart's role as host and executive producer meant he was tired all the time, especially due to his habit of micromanaging every last detail, not only of the show but also of the employees. "He asks about every tiny detail of things that are important in your life," said Smithberg, "and he isn't feigning. He knows the eating habits of everyone, and he knows when all the camera guys are pooping."

And then came September 11, 2001. Perhaps Stewart's finest moment came in a moment of horror and poignancy and great uncertainty for the future of *The Daily Show*.

It had seemed like just another Tuesday morning. He and Tracey had recently celebrated their first wedding anniversary, and he was getting ready to head uptown from their Soho apartment to the studio to start working on that night's show when he heard a thundering crash.

Then he looked out the window and saw one of the World Trade Center towers on fire. Twenty minutes later, they grabbed the cat carriers and a few belongings, and evacuated their apartment, heading uptown.

And then a horrible thought occurred to him:

How could he be funny at a time like this? And how could the show possibly continue?

"Everyone was so scared and on tenterhooks," said Brian

Farnham, editor-in-chief of *Time Out New York*. "How could you be funny about something that was so terrifying? Jon Stewart and *The Daily Show* were one of the first shows to say, 'You know you can make fun of anything if you do it the right way.'"

"It was a fragile time for everything," Stewart acknowledged. "People talk about the Holocaust as the greatest inhumane times. But my guess is that even at Auschwitz people were telling jokes. It's human nature to find light in darkness somehow."

During the first week after the terrorist attacks, the networks and many cable channels pulled their regularly scheduled programming to focus on airing news updates and live broadcasts from Ground Zero. On September 17, David Letterman was the first of the late-night talk shows to return to the air. *The Daily Show* went back on the air on September 20, and Stewart began the show without the music, without the roaming cameras, and without the wildly cheering audience.

It was one of the best monologues of his life, which he delivered in a stilted yet straightforward manner without his typical slightly ramped-up tone. Throughout the almost nine-minute talk, Stewart occasionally had to pause to regain his composure. The funny man was nowhere in sight. "They said to get back to work, and there were no jobs available for a man in the fetal position," he said. "We sit in the back and we throw spitballs—never forgetting the fact that it is a luxury in this country that allows us to do that.

"The view from my apartment was the World Trade Center. Now it's gone. They attacked it. This symbol of American ingenuity and strength and labor and imagination and commerce and it is gone. But you know what the view is now? The Statue of Liberty. The view from the south of Manhattan is now the Statue of Liberty. You can't beat that."

He's said that he only watched the segment once, and that he vowed never to watch it again, it was too painful.

Over the nine days that the *Show* didn't air, a quarter of viewers passed up the reruns and switched to channels that offered more hospitable comfort-food kinds of shows, like Nick at Nite. But after the new shows resumed, not only did regular viewers return but new ones watched as well, in part because Stewart was intent on serving as a teacher of sorts, to teach viewers about certain elements of this strange new fragile world while still conveying it through the lens of humor.

And his image and influence changed from that point on.

CHAPTER 8

OUR ENTIRE DAY is focused on taking the un-fun we have and turning it into fun when it gets on the air," said Stewart. "Because we function, actually, very similarly probably to a news show in that we have sort of an editorial meeting in the morning. It's a really structured day. We actually do have a very good time doing it, but it's sort of relentless, and the structure of our day is a lot more rigid, I think, than people would imagine."

Looking at a day in the life at *The Daily Show* reveals that putting together each program is a never-ending process. The first bit of work starts around 7 A.M. when a team of producers settles in and starts to review TiVo'ed videos and news stories from the day before for potential images, sound bites, and stories that would make good fodder for that evening's show. They also thumb through all three of the local New York papers— the *Post* is "our paper of record" according to one writer—for ideas and obscure and entertaining news stories as well. In addition, several television sets broadcast live feeds from all of the morning news shows from ABC, NBC, CBS, and cable networks like CNN and Fox News.

The writers start to wander in shortly before 9 A.M. when they gather in the writers' lounge for a meeting that is known around the studio as "our morning cup of sadness." That first hour is basically spent cracking jokes about the major news stories from the previous day while munching on bagels from H&H, a long-established New York bakery. It's during that crucial hour when the first nuggets start to emerge. "We get specific about what angles we'll be taking and we've all agreed to," said writer J. R. Havlan. "We're joking around from nine to ten, and those jokes frequently end up on the show."

The team then breaks up to start writing that night's show. Here, the joking out loud basically ceases as the writers focus on the task at hand. They are able to crank out a first draft of that night's show in about ninety minutes. "We know exactly what we need to get done at any period of time," said writer Jason Ross. "We've seen the videos and we know there are four good sound bites for the story. It's pretty laid out for you."

Producer Rory Albanese, for one, marvels at the writers' speed. "They're really fast and real good about it," he said, adding that, as is the case with anything, practice enhances both skill and speed. "You get better at it. It's a muscle and you work it out. It gets stronger."

"You get good at knowing what you need to attack," Havlan added.

Around 11:30, producers and research staff start to gather the scripts from the writers so they can begin to do their work, from selecting news clips to run alongside Stewart's comments to locating props—occasionally making them from scratch—to accompany a monologue or sketch.

The next three hours pass in a blur as Stewart and the production team edit and tighten the scripts, further refine the jokes, and offer up suggestions to the research staff. Along the way, the tech staff plans their camera angles and video shifts, altering them with each new script draft that comes in.

The Daily Show writers and producers also have to be careful not to duplicate anything going on at *The Colbert Report*, which spun off from *The Daily Show* in 2005. Despite the distinct tone of the two shows, there is bound to be at least some crossover. "The game they're playing is a slightly different one from us, so we don't trip on each other that much," said Stewart. "And let's put it this way: This ain't the Serengeti. There's plenty of food to go around."

When Ben Karlin was executive producer of both shows, he visited the two studios several times a day to check for any duplication. For example, when the Mark Foley sex scandal first broke in the fall of 2006, in which the Republican congressman from Florida sent explicit notes to a sixteen-year-old male page, Karlin green-lighted stories for both shows.

The Daily Show take: "It's the Jewish Day of Atonement," said Stewart. "I don't know how many days of fasting can get you out of trying to bang sixteen-year-olds. My guess is at least three days. Even after that, probably a month of salads."

Colbert, on the other hand, said that the media had gotten it all wrong about Foley, explaining that "stud" really stands for "Strong Teenager Using Democracy" in text-message shorthand, and that "horny" is short for "Happy On Reaching New Year's."

"Every January first," he said, "that is the message I send to my buddies at Stephen Colbert's Youth Camp for Young Studs: 'I am incredibly horny.'"

Because Stewart serves as executive producer for *The Colbert Report*, he also reviews scripts for both shows before nailing them into the schedule. "He looks at our scripts, and helps us to see where to find the most fruit," said Colbert. "His instincts are maddeningly good, and I don't recommend going to the mat with him over a comedic idea. We actually talk way more now than we did when we worked together, because I now understand how difficult his job is, to executive produce and then to be the ultimate writing voice of everything that gets said. I need someone's advice, so I call fairly frequently."

While this frenzy is going on, part of the staff is out in the field working with correspondents to tape their segments, or working on projects that take longer to produce. According to executive producer D. J. Javerbaum, despite the luxury of time that these projects have, very often they're just not as funny as the pieces done on the fly in a matter of hours. "Pieces thrown together in twenty-four to forty-eight hours often come out better than the ones you plan more," he said.

Writers, researchers, and producers will pop in and out of Stewart's office right up until rehearsal begins at four o'clock. First there's a rough rehearsal where the writers, producers, and Stewart are listening and still tinkering with each word, image, prop, and nuance. Then they run through it again.

"In the studio, you do one rough run-through, where you're bad and you flub your words and then squeegee the sweat off your eyebrows and do it again," said Lauren Weedman, who worked as a correspondent from 2001 to 2002. "The first one is a stumble-through, and it is petrifying."

"There are definitely moments in rehearsal where we go, 'Wow, that's a little strident, we might want to dial that down a bit,'" Stewart admitted.

"Very often it feels like you're doing the five or eleven o'clock news because things are changing so rapidly and Jon wants to go as close to six o'clock as possible," said director Rob Feld. "Once he puts that suit on at a quarter to four, he's in show mode, and everybody feeds off that. It's not live but you don't want to screw up because he's sitting in the chair and you don't want to have to do the joke twice [during taping] since the audience has already seen it. You want to do your best for him because he's bringing his triple-A game every time."

After the rehearsal ends, a feverish flurry of rewrites ensue, and then, no matter what kind of shape the script and performers are in, the audience begins to file into the studio around 5:30; some people have waited outside the building on line since the morning. A warm-up comedian will spend fifteen minutes or so cracking jokes and prompting the audience on protocol—no talking, texting, or Tweeting on cell phones, no recording the show, and no photographs—as well as the proper way to laugh: outwardly, not the snickering way you might laugh at home while watching the show. And just before the cameras start to roll, Stewart walks onto the stage and takes a few questions from the audience: "You can ask me anything you like, and I will answer you facetiously" is his standard introductory line. During the Q&A session—which can last ten to fifteen minutes—audience members ask everything from how many researchers he has on staff to his honest thoughts about Bill O'Reilly. Occasionally someone will go on a tear about conspiracy theories, but there are a bevy of staffers in the aisles specifically used to cut these rants short.

The show zooms by, and by the time that "Your Moment of Zen" runs, the editors have already begun to cut and shape the episode into a cohesive whole. Stewart runs through a brief postmortem with the staff, which elicits typical comments.

Not everyone can handle the pressure of what is required to make each show, let alone deal with the exacting standards of Stewart. While many staffers have quit due to the pressure over the years, others have decided to leave because of Stewart himself, who "is a man of very high and almost impossible expectations at times, but we try to meet them because we love the guy," stage manager Craig Spinney cagily replied to a question about his boss's demeanor behind the scenes.

"It's a harsh work environment," said Havlan.

For his part, one way in which *The Daily Show* does take after traditional news broadcasts is that the role of the anchor is not only to deliver the news but to act as a kind of managing editor in the staff structure.

"The last thing I think about is performing," said Stewart. "It's all about the managing, editing, and moving toward showtime."

Even though the daily deadline could be crushing at times, Stewart admitted that being a fake news show means their deadlines are more loosey-goosey than in a straight news show, while also helping to provide the unique *Daily Show* twist to a story.

"It's been exciting to see fake news catching on like that," he added. "We don't make things up, we just distill it to hopefully its most humorous nugget. And in that sense it seems faked and skewed just because we don't have to be subjective or pretend to be objective. We can just put it out there."

Despite what others say of his exacting standards, Stewart claims he's perfectly at home delegating much of the responsibility for getting the show on the air to his staff. "I can literally show up at five o'clock pretty drunk, and as long as the show is spelled out phonetically on the prompter, I'll do OK," he said. "I just have to face in the right direction."

After the frenzy and intense focus required to create, edit, and polish a completed twenty-two-minute show every day, the aftermath of the rehearsal and taping before a live audience allows Stewart to let his hair down. After all, the hard work is basically done by the time five o'clock rolls around.

"A lot of times, Jon goes through rehearsals with his feet up on the desk," said Havlan.

After providing the framework and general guidelines to the writers, editors, and correspondents, Stewart treats them the same way that Comedy Central treats *The Daily Show*: he gives them a very long leash. "Jon taught me how to do [political comedy] so it would be smart," said Colbert. "He encouraged everyone to have a point of view and there had to be a thought behind every joke."

Though the planning, writing, and rewriting can be killer, one feature that Stewart calls the one-to-one is almost too easy. "I'm sure that guy fucking said the exact opposite thing six months ago," Stewart or a staffer will say in response to a quote from a politician or celebrity in a recent news story. Then a writer or production assistant will be off and running, assisted by TiVo to find the opposite quote that they'll run back to back. "If you can get a one-to-one with a guy saying the exact opposite of what he said today, then you . . . giggle."

While he heaps accolades on top of accolades when it comes

to his staff, Stewart has a particular regard for his executive producer Ben Karlin, who came to the show from *The Onion*, though they do have stylistic differences when it comes to humor. If anything, Karlin's brand of humor is harsher and more pointed while Stewart prefers to concentrate on the precise combination of words and jokes that will bring the biggest laugh from the audience.

Once he got past the first year, Stewart said it helped to think of the show as doing a twenty-two-minute stand-up routine, where the goal was to fit twenty good jokes into each episode. He admits that's what makes it relatively easy. "The concept is to come up with a wisecrack every forty-five seconds, [which is] the only thing that I've been trained for."

After producing the show for a couple of years, Stewart had relaxed into a rhythm—perhaps a little too much. Many guests—not just politicians—were often caught off guard by how unprepared Stewart was. When author David Halberstam appeared on the show, Stewart revealed his hand when he was wrapping up the segment. "It's a beautiful read, and, as always, great to see you."

The problem: just two minutes earlier, Stewart told the author that he hadn't even cracked open the book. Plus it was Halberstam's first appearance on the show, and the first time he and Stewart had met.

"But we've never met before!" said Halberstam, at first slightly shocked but then dissolving into laughter.

Stewart later admitted that he felt bad about the interview, but not that much.

In fact, Oscar-winning actress Jennifer Lawrence teased him about his sloppy interviewing techniques when she appeared on the show in the fall of 2013.

"Your producers and everyone involved in the show tell everyone, 'He's not really gonna know a lot about the movie or about you,'" Lawrence humorously scolded him on the November 21 show when he admitted he wasn't very familiar with her current film, *The Hunger Games: Catching Fire*.

"Normally you have like a pre-interview and you kinda go over like bullet points of things we want to touch on," she said. "The producers are like, 'No, no, you guys are just gonna talk. He's just probably not gonna ask you anything about the movie. He might not ask you anything.'"

True to form, Stewart admitted as much on the air, though he was visibly surprised at being called out by the young actress during taping. "I don't prepare for these very well," he said.

But despite the Halberstam incident, Stewart does try to read the books of the authors whom he hosts on the show. "Some weeks we have four books [on the show] and they can be thick ones and [sometimes] historical nonfiction," he said. "But I read pretty quickly, and I try and read as much of the books as I possibly can. I have a pretty good ability of getting through it and retaining a good deal of its information for a four- to six-hour period."

Despite the fact that Stewart typically treats non-politician guests in a lighthearted manner, occasionally he turns the tide and becomes outwardly hostile toward a guest. Sometimes the parts don't make the final edited broadcast—and only hit the news when Stewart later makes an offhanded remark about a past guest—but sometimes they do.

Take Hugh Grant, whom Stewart has referred to as the worst guest he's ever hosted, adding "and we've had dictators on the show." Grant appeared on the show to promote his movie

Did You Hear About the Morgans?, and from the moment he set foot in the studio, the actor became extremely demanding and complained pretty much nonstop. "He's giving everyone shit the whole time, and he's a big pain in the ass," said Stewart. When Grant openly grumbled to some staffers about the movie snippet that would appear during the segment, saying, "What is that clip? It's a terrible clip!" Stewart let him have it.

"Well, then, make a better fucking movie," he replied.

The exchange was understandably cut from the final broadcast, but made headlines later on when a reporter asked Stewart about his all-time least favorite guest. And then Grant himself commented on their exchange, actually admitting via Twitter that Stewart wasn't too far off the mark. "Turns out my inner crab got the better of me with TV producer in 09," he tweeted. "Unforgivable. J Stewart correct to give me kicking."

The offices of *The Daily Show* on the west side of Manhattan were at 513 West 54th Street, before they moved to the new studios at 733 Third Avenue between 51st and 52nd Streets in 2005 because *The Colbert Report* had taken over the 54th Street facilities. The environment could best be described as a utilitarian office setting with a comedic, almost frat-boy feel to it. A visitor once described it as "a narrow, carpeted hallway with a series of small offices that could be singles and doubles in a freshman dorm." The doors to each office are typically covered with a variety of small bulletin boards, games, and dolls and cartoon characters, along with a smattering of newspaper stories.

Competition was fierce to get a job on *The Daily Show*—producers regularly reviewed résumés and clips from writers, comedians, and administrative staff whether they were sent cold or via another staff member—but perhaps it was even more breakneck among college students to land an internship on the show. After all, they were the *Show*'s most loyal audience. Thousands of applications poured in for the six internships offered each summer on the show.

As a broadcast journalism major at the Edward R. Murrow School of Communications at Washington State University, John Obrien won an internship to the show in the summer of 2002. Most interns came from a comedy background; he felt that his application stood out because of his journalism major. Though he was thrilled at winning the position, he was also warned that his days would be filled with lots of gofer tasks like making copies, messengering tapes, and running all over Manhattan getting props for the show; indeed, on his first day, even though he was unfamiliar with New York, a production coordinator asked him to go to Spanish Harlem to buy a bright orange tank top in size 7-XL at a hole-in-the-wall convenience store. He was also informed that he would have very little contact—if any—with Stewart or the correspondents.

At the time, there were about forty people working at *The Daily Show*, and Obrien described the working environment as incredibly relaxed. "It wasn't a pressure cooker at all," he said. "People brought their dogs to work, there were frequent office parties, and overall, it was very loose," he said.

Seth Zimmerman interned with Obrien at *The Daily Show* in the summer of 2002, and he remembers watching Colbert and Carell review a script for their "Even Stepvhen" debate, where each correspondent takes an opposing side of a timely and often controversial subject. Sometimes they'd rehearse it in the interview room, other times they'd go over it backstage.

"It was cool to see the two of them go over an 'Even Stepvhen' scene because they made it look like they'd been doing this forever," said Zimmerman. "They seemed so natural but also so iconic. They were always hitting a button of some kind, and they'd always laugh. Once they got on camera, of course, they'd be totally professional, but beforehand they'd both turn it on and off at will as they tinkered with the sketch. Then backstage, right before they went out, they'd toss a football back and forth."

Every day, the interns rotated within several departments, ranging from general production to post-production audience, to working even with the writers or in accounting. Mandy Ganis was a *Daily Show* intern in the summer of 2003. "We were all working in such small quarters, so we got to see everyone all the time and talk with everyone," she said. "They weren't big names, they were friendly and laid-back."

The humor on the show naturally extended throughout the rest of the office, including the intracorporate documents, a weekly newsletter, and the bible for new interns: *The Intern's Guide to The Daily Show.* The handbook gave them everything they needed to know for their tenure, and was written with typical *Daily Show* humor. A job description for each staff member was listed, along with the location of his/her office. For instance, Jon Stewart's office was located on the second floor, and this was his job description: "Hosts, writes, consults, manages the Bennigan's off of exit 7 on the Jersey Turnpike."

Ganis soon learned that when it came to the administrative staff, writers, and on-air talent at the show, the most valuable intern was whoever was the general production intern that day, whose primary job was to buy food to stock the entire office, including the green room, the control room, the writers' lounge, and the kitchen. The list was preprinted and long, with around fifty different items to inventory and check off before heading to D'Agostino, the supermarket around the block.

The list included the following:

- Three boxes of cookies for the control room
- Three bags of candy for the green room
- Soy milk—vanilla if they have it
- Seven blocks of Philadelphia cream cheese
- Three Fuji apples
- Three boxes of Kleenex (unscented)
- Lucky Charms EVERY DAY

The intern in charge of the shopping was supposed to first check to see if anything needed replacing; if, for instance, there were only two Fuji apples in the house, the intern would buy one more that day.

Food responsibilities were not limited to the general production intern. For the intern assigned to the writers' lounge, the first order of business was "to bring the writers' bagel basket up at 9:30 and bring it back down to the kitchen between 10:30 and 10:45."

The intern's primary responsibility boiled down to the care and feeding of the writers.

. . .

Besides the food, one of the first things that stand out at the studio are the dogs.

Lots of them.

One of the perks of working at *The Daily Show* is that employees are allowed to bring their dogs to work, which contributes to the somewhat relaxing atmosphere. While not everyone brings their own dog to work every day—including Stewart—at least four or five will be on hand at any one time. Stewart will sometimes bring his pit bulls in.

But it's not just fun and games. "We all feel this responsibility to keep the dogs pretty well-behaved," said Jen Flanz, a co-executive producer of the show who is often accompanied by Parker, her Lab mix. "If someone comes in and thinks this is a free-for-all, they would be mistaken."

Supervising producer Tim Greenberg often brings his rescue Pointer-mix named Ally to the studio, and agrees with Flanz. "Like the show itself, there really is a strict discipline underlying what looks like a free-form," he said. "This is a giant dog playground. The dogs run around, and there are at least eight to ten treat stations throughout the office. Ally's got her own schedule of things she does. She gets exercise running up and back. The only thing that would make it better is if there were grass and squirrels [inside]."

According to Hillary Kun, supervising producer and the show's talent booker, "the dogs loosen up the place. Personally, if I have a bad day, or am stressed, it's nice having the company of the dogs, to have them come into my office. Dogs are therapeutic."

"We have animals around to help us relax a little, reminders that you shouldn't take life too seriously," added correspondent Wyatt Cenac.

"The dogs that get to work at this office have won the dog lottery," said Justin Chabot, artistic coordinator and DV shooter.

"I feel like I'm that much harder to get rid of because the guy who runs the show loves Ally," Greenberg jokes.

At least once, the office dogs have made it onto the air. In January 2009, Anderson Cooper conducted a dog debate—tagged as a *Puppedential* debate in a series called "Road to the Doghouse"—to help the Obamas pick the best dog to live in the White House.

The dogs in the office have had a kind of chain reaction effect. Formerly dog-free employees who end up spending a lot of the workday around dogs will often go out and adopt one of their own. Former correspondent John Oliver is one of them. He adopted a golden retriever puppy named Hoagie in late 2011 because "she really doesn't give a shit about *The Daily Show*, which I find enormously helpful at the end of the day."

He brought her to the studio one day when she was still a puppy, but she became so excited by the other dogs that she just wanted to play, and that created problems for Oliver when he was under deadline.

With that said, he is grateful for the canine company. "I don't know what we would do without these dogs," he said. That difference was made clear one day when Pervez Musharraf, the former president of Pakistan, was a guest on the show and a memo went out the day before that all staff dogs had to stay home because of the bomb-sniffing dogs that would be checking the place out before Musharraf's arrival.

"We could really feel the difference when they weren't here," said Oliver. "It would be a very different place if there weren't dogs walking around."

Though *Daily Show* staffers first started to bring their dogs to work during the Craig Kilborn era, Stewart has done his part to actively encourage it, with a few limits. "It makes for a very nice environment," he said. "There are rules and everybody has to be responsible. You gotta potty train them. You gotta make sure that if there are issues with other dogs that they are dealt with the right way."

The combination of dogs roaming through the halls and the free food available created an uncomfortable situation for a period of time. "We went through a period where we had to tell people to stop feeding the dogs off the catering table, because six months into it, everybody looked like Dom DeLuise!" said Stewart. "The dogs were just lying on the floor, bloated, and ready to pass out. So we've instituted some discipline, but it's really nice to have them around."

In addition to helping the employees feel better, the dogs also make guests, some of which have included Jennifer Aniston, Ricky Gervais, and Betty White, feel more at ease before they head out in front of the camera for a segment with Jon. When Senator Barack Obama made his first appearance on the show, he immediately sprawled on the floor to commune with the dogs.

"As a comedian, there's a lot of love you get from an audience's laughter and applause," said Bob Wiltfong, who worked as a *Daily Show* correspondent from 2004 to 2005. "As a professional comedian, it's my theory that people get into comedy because there's something missing in their own personal life, and they need that void filled through laughter and acceptance onstage."

"Some of the most miserable people I've ever met are comedy people," he noted, though he added that Colbert was one of the rare exceptions. "It made for an interesting dynamic at *The Daily Show*, which had some of the smartest, funniest people I've known, all moving toward one common goal, but the flip side was that there were a lot of miserable curmudgeonly people working there. In general, comedy just isn't an environment that lends itself toward happiness."

"It's like a dysfunctional family," said Lewis Black.

Even though it's their job to be funny, the pressure of meeting a regular nightly deadline as well as constantly trying to figure out where you are in the pecking order takes its toll on people putting together a comedy show, whether they're writers or on-air talent. Wiltfong also noticed the different ways in which Jon and Stephen approached their jobs. "What you see on air with both those guys is pretty much what they're like off air," he said. "In order for Jon to do some of the comedy on *The Daily Show* for so many years and for it to be high quality, it has to come from a place of anger, because then it's truly biting and gets at the truth. In real life he's not a ball of laughs, because he's pretty upset about what's going on in the world."

"Colbert is the total opposite of Jon," he continued. "He's very upbeat and personable. He'll call out something and say, 'Can you believe this is going on?' while Jon is more like, 'These assholes, look what they're doing, let's rake these guys over the coals and make it smart and funny because these guys are doing stupid stuff.'"

The two comics, of course, have their own takes on things.

"Jon deconstructs the news, he's ironic and detached," said Colbert, "while I falsely construct the news and I'm ironically attached, I'm not detached at all, I'm passionate about what I'm talking about. I illustrate the hypocrisy of a news item as a *character*. So while Jon's just being Jon on the show, conversely, that's me *not* being me, that's me being that Stephen Colbert guy."

When it comes to politics, comedians tend to be iconoclasts, and anti–status quo. "Jon is admirably balanced," Colbert continued. "Every time I work with him on something, he tries to perceive the true intention of the person speaking, left or right, regardless of whether it was something he believed in or not. He wants to *honestly* mock."

In the end, however, they're both after the same thing: "Basically, it's a bunch of guys exchanging ideas, laughing about stuff, and getting excited about smart funny ideas," said Wiltfong.

It didn't take Colbert long to break out of the pack of correspondents. He filled in for Jon as guest host on *The Daily Show* for the first time on January 24, 2001.

Although Jon and Stephen spent a lot of time working and laughing at the studio, their friendship was mostly limited to the office. "In theory, I think Jon would be excellent company," said Colbert. "But I have nothing to back it up."

"The biggest mistake that people make is thinking that Jon and Stephen sit down before every show and say, okay, how are we going to change the world, or some bullshit like that," said Karlin. "They both really just want to get a laugh."

Even though he preceded Stewart on the show, Colbert admires and looks up to the host. "Jon's very generous and treats me like a peer," he said. "I think I still think of him as an older brother, he comes before I do, he has bigger numbers, it's hard to do a strip show, he's taught me a lot, how not to worry about what goes on outside the building and just get our work done every day."

As the mutual love fest continued over the years, some at the *Show* noticed that they began to shut others out. "One negative aspect of working with Colbert from the perspective of the other correspondents was that he was very tight with Jon," said Wiltfong. "Jon and Stephen were always very friendly and chummy with each other; on set or during rehearsals they were the best of friends, but it was an unusual occurrence when other correspondents engaged Jon in conversation."

On election night in 2004, all the correspondents were in the studio for the live broadcast. During the rehearsal, the correspondents sat in a corner while Stephen and Jon sat at the desk bullshitting with each other, making no attempt at conversation with the others. "It always seemed like a world we couldn't get into, and it always struck me as curious," said Wiltfong. "I didn't know why that dynamic existed and I wasn't the only one. Ed Helms and I are relatively friendly and we talked about that, but Jon just doesn't let many people in and Stephen was one of the few."

Part of the problem, unvoiced among some, was that the close relationship between Stewart and Colbert—along with an increase in Colbert's guest host appearances—meant that it was clear who was going to be next in line, who was already succeeding more than the rest. "There was grumbling among fellow comedians that you don't want to see another comedian succeed because it means less laughter and stage time for you," said Wiltfong. "That's part of the business."

In addition to clearly favoring Colbert over the other correspondents, it was an open secret that women staffers were in short supply on *The Daily Show*, at least in the writers' room, which was, after all, where much of the spin and overall tone of the show was set.

When Olivia Munn first went on the air as a *Daily Show* correspondent in 2010, she was the first new female correspondent to be hired—or at least the first to make it past the freelance correspondent stage—since 2001 when Samantha Bee had joined, and who was still filing regular reports in 2014. Despite her longevity, Bee admitted that she found the atmosphere uncomfortable at times.

"She struggled with being the only woman on the show in what is a male-dominated industry to begin with," said Wiltfong, who shared an office with Bee when he was on the show. "She felt like the low person on the totem pole, and that's not a good thing to feel as a performer."

Lauren Weedman also worked on the show as an on-air correspondent from 2001 to 2002. (Though correspondents are "hired," they're only paid for each report that airs.) "I was told when I was hired that they have a very hard time finding and keeping women, and that I was lucky to get a one-year contract," she said.

She added that hearing her coworkers' comments didn't help. "Everyone kept saying, 'It's sooo hard to keep women here,'" she said.

Some felt that Weedman had a distinct disadvantage going

in: her comic schtick was essentially that of a very annoying woman. "My comedy came from being kind of insecure, broken, needy, neurotic," she explained. "And that works in a group of guys if you're a nerdy, insecure guy and you can all just banter away. But if you're a woman, it's harder to be that person without some support."

Whether it was from nerves from being on national TV, being a little bit starstruck, or just her personality, Weedman's routine spilled over into the office atmosphere, where it was clear that given the stress of producing a tightly planned show on an even tighter schedule, Stewart had no time or inclination to deal with what he viewed as a problem employee. Whether Stewart had a deaf ear toward certain kinds of comedy or whether he just didn't like having a female correspondent with Weedman's style around the office was unclear, but Stewart's makeup person told Weedman that he had definite issues with her, suggesting that he thought she was making fun of him. "'He can't tell that you're kidding,'" she said. "'I've known him a long time and I just think he doesn't get your kidding. I would go right now and talk to him. Like how you talk to me. Like how you talk to everyone but him.'"

Weedman spoke with Stewart, who apparently alleviated her concern, but the constant stream of women coming into the studio each day on auditions told her otherwise. "They were always having auditions for women," she said. "I would see all these blond women coming in—they'd give them the same copy they gave me the night before. And I knew I'd be fired."

Soon enough, she was fired, though according to what one colleague told her, her termination had nothing to do with her talent or her approach to comedy.

"One of the issues that got in the way of my success on the

show was that I just wasn't as cute as the other female report-ers," said Weedman. That colleague apparently told her, "I'm not saying that I don't think you're cute. I'm just talking about guys, the fans of the show, the American people, and all the Comedy Central executives."

"Did I feel like there was a boys' club there?" Stacey Grenrock-Woods, a former correspondent on the show from 1999 through 2003, asked rhetorically. "Yeah, sure. Did I want to be part of it? Not necessarily. So it kind of goes both ways."

Hallie Haglund, who started working as a *Daily Show* writer in 2009 after working in several other positions on the show since 2006, offered another perspective. "I do think there is a huge element of shared experience," she said. "So much of our show is comic book shit that I have no idea what people are talking about, or something from *Star Wars* I've never seen. And I can come in and help out on *Sex and the City* guest ques-tions like I did yesterday."

Maybe the only women who could succeed in writing late-night comedy have a thick skin or grew up in a house full of brothers . . . or both.

Writer Jonathan Bines helped launch *Jimmy Kimmel Live* in 2003, and even he admitted that "late-night writers' rooms are not fabulous places to be. They're miserable for everyone." But that doesn't mean female comedians don't want to be there, and those who make it in the door know what they're getting into.

"That's what's fun, that's why we get into comedy: to mess around with comedians all day," said Ali Waller.

"If you're not comfortable with sexual humor or with crude-ness or with . . . people being really honest about certain emo-tions, then . . . this job is not for you," said Daley Haggar, a female comedy writer whose résumé includes *The Big Bang Theory* and *South Park*.

"It's a very aggressive medium, and it's not the medium for fragile flowers," said Janis Hirsch, a veteran comedy writer whose résumé includes *Frasier, Modern Family*, and *Will & Grace*. "It's a job, it's not a perfect world. Women have to either nut up and get into the spirit of it or not look for a job on a show that's all about men."

To be sure, female writers have never been found in great quantities on most late-night talk shows. And 80 percent of late-night hosts are male, Chelsea Handler being the exception. "When you're writing for late night, you're writing through one person's prism, and that person at the shows you're looking at is always a dude," said Hallie Haglund.

"It's the law of averages," said Lizz Winstead. "More guys than women are in comedy." In fact, when she and Smithberg started *The Daily Show* in the pre–Jon Stewart days and solicited writers to work on the show, they received over a hundred résumés, but "only about three or four were from women."

So while former female employees and correspondents—as well as members of the general public—may often complain about the boys' club at the show, the truth is that the atmosphere behind the scenes at *The Daily Show* is not that different from other talk shows of its ilk. And given the cutthroat competition to snag a job at one of these highly popular programs, there will always be another person—male or female—willing to put their concerns aside in order to become part of a successful and visible franchise.

.   .   .

In addition to women on the show feeling slighted, some critics of the show believed that the overall tone of *The Daily Show* sometimes crossed an unnecessary line in the name of comedy, verging on the edge of nastiness just to get a laugh. Stewart disagreed wholeheartedly.

"We rarely do ad hominem attacks," said Stewart. "In general, it's based in frustration over reality."

"We claim no respectability," added Colbert. "There's no status I would not surrender for a joke, so we don't have to defend anything."

At the same time, even though the overall tone of *The Daily Show* is satirical, "The show is our own personal beliefs," said Stewart. "That's the only reason why we go to work every day. You try not to let it become didactic, you always remember it's a comedy show more than a political satire, but we very much infuse it with who we are."

Though he had no straightforward news reporting experience, Stewart thought he approached his work in the same spirit, if not sometimes better than the professionals. "I think what we do is relatively well thought out," he said. "And while there are times we step over a line when things are happening fast and furious, the truth is, as fake journalists, we exercise far more restraint than the journalists I see." He cited how the media handled the aftermath of the Columbine shootings, where TV crews essentially mobbed students and their families. "I had never seen anything like that," he noted. "We didn't make one joke about it, so as far as our comedy being in the depths, I think we've got a long way to go toward the bottom until we take on the actual ethics of real journalism."

"He doesn't want to rip the curtain back and let people

see that there is medicine being delivered here," said Devin Gordon, formerly a senior writer at *Newsweek*. "He also doesn't want to sound too pompous and say, 'Hey, I'm just telling jokes.' They just happen to be about the headlines, but anybody who watches the show knows that there is a core of anger that is driving the entire enterprise."

And sometimes that anger is unleashed on the staff. Comedian David Feldman worked as a writer on *The Daily Show* and his memories of Stewart are anything but warm and fuzzy. "In my opinion, Stewart is very manipulative," he said. "He's a crowd pleaser and [only] gives the *illusion* of taking chances. I'm a staunch member of the Writer's Guild of America and Jon Stewart fought his writers when they wanted to go union [in late 2006]. They went union and [he] has been punishing them ever since. If you watch the show, he doesn't really do well-crafted jokes. He'll throw a couple in, but it's mostly mugging and shouting. He's funny, but he's punishing his writers. He doesn't use his writers' stuff because he's mad at them for going union."

"My boss is like if you took Willy Wonka and mixed him with Hitler," added correspondent Ed Helms in one *Daily Show* segment, but he delivered the line in a way that it looked like at least part of him wasn't joking. "He's crazy like Willy Wonka and he's psycho like Hitler. But he doesn't have a mustache."

Writers are not the only ones with stories to tell. A staffer recalls the time when Stewart's temper got the better of him and he hurled a newspaper at Smithberg during a story meeting while screaming inches away from her face. He later excused his behavior by saying, "Sorry, that was the bad Jon . . . I try not to let him out."

"When I tell people that I used to work for Jon . . . they ask . . . , 'Oh, is he nice?' " said former *Daily Show* correspondent Stacey Grenrock-Woods. "Now, I would never think of Jon Stewart as 'nice.' He's a comedian, and comedians aren't always particularly nice people. But these people look so hopeful. . . . So I always say, 'Yes, he's very nice.' And they always say, 'Oh, thank God. I don't know what I'd do if he wasn't.' "

"There's a huge discrepancy between the Jon Stewart who goes on TV every night and the Jon Stewart who runs *The Daily Show* with joyless rage," said an anonymous former executive.

It was something that Bob Wiltfong witnessed on a daily basis during his tenure at the show, and he blames Stewart's tendency toward anger as one of the reasons why he only worked there a short time. "When I look at the show now, I can see the anger come out in his comedy, and I'm not like that," he said. "I'm much more positive about the world. So in a way, I didn't fit the core principle there."

Indeed, when it surfaces publicly, Stewart's anger has seemed misplaced and just a little bit self-righteous. Actor and comedian Seth MacFarlane created *Family Guy*, among other top-rated comedy shows, and right after the 2006–2007 writers' strike, he incorporated a brief snippet—a very inside-the-industry joke—into the animated show that ragged on Stewart for going back on the air while the writers were still out on strike. After the *Family Guy* episode aired, Stewart called Mac-Farlane and proceeded to scream and yell at him for a full hour, saying he had no right to call him out for that.

"I was really kind of in shock more than anything else,"

MacFarlane told Piers Morgan on CNN. "It was kind of an odd Hollywood moment. I was a huge fan of his show, and here I was getting this angry phone call." MacFarlane added that Stewart then asked him, "Who the hell made you the moral arbiter of Hollywood?"

Morgan then replied, "But not if you're the self-appointed moral arbiter of Hollywood, which is exactly the position he plays. There's a certain irony in Jon Stewart ringing up haranguing you for mocking him."

Then again, perhaps Morgan was just getting back at Stewart for the time a year earlier when Stewart appeared on Larry King's show on CNN and criticized the network's decision to bring in Morgan to take over King's show; after all, MacFarlane was visibly shocked when Morgan initially brought up the angry phone call on his show. Before then, he hadn't mentioned it publicly.

Even after the first few years, the *Daily Show* schedule was so relentless and taxing, more than a few staffers wondered how long Stewart could keep it up. "Doing *The Daily Show with Jon Stewart* is creatively and physically exhausting," he admitted just six months after starting as host in 1999. Yet, at the same time, he admitted that exhaustion had its benefits.

Our work "is actually enhanced by a certain sleep deprivation, because it's the part of your brain that you're not really in touch with until something's desperately wrong," he said.

"There are a lot of days when we walk off that show and go, 'Ewww, we were putrid,'" he said. "I feel like when you watch that show, it shouldn't look like we're working hard on it, but we are."

He'd worked his tail off to get the opportunity to host the

show, and once there he'd be damned if he'd let anything or anyone interfere. But even he admitted that sometimes he thought it was too much. "Even if you're eating delicious chocolate cake, there are moments you feel like, 'I've had too much,'" he said. "Now replace 'chocolate cake' with 'shit taco' and you know what our day is like every day."

CHAPTER 9

Wɪᴛʜ *Tʜᴇ Dᴀɪʟʏ Sʜᴏᴡ* firmly established as a ratings success, Stewart started to branch out from his hosting and producing duties. In 2003, the clause in his Comedy Central contract about doing no outside work had long expired, and he decided to test the waters once more in Hollywood. He accepted a role in the movie *Death to Smoochy*, which came out in 2002.

The movie, directed by Danny DeVito and starring Ed Norton and Robin Williams, came out in the spring of 2002 and was pitched as a black comedy featuring child entertainers that also offered a thinly veiled satirical critique of Barney the dinosaur, a popular children's character of the time. The plot revolved around children's TV show host Randolph Smiley—played by Robin Williams—and his desire to exact revenge upon his replacement—a purple rhinoceros named Smoochy, played by Edward Norton—after getting fired from the show. In keeping with Stewart's previous track record with movies, the critics savaged it.

"The script is so shoddy, the direction so inept, and the

Stewart and Vincent Schiavelli in a scene from the 2002 movie *Death to Smoochy*. *(Courtesy REX USA/Snap Stills/Rex)*

acting so wretched, that every second of this film creaks like a broken-down tractor," wrote one critic, who added that it was the first time in his life that he had walked out of a movie theater before a film had ended.

For his part, Stewart admitted that he had bombed in the role of Marion Frank Stokes—president of the TV network that aired the show and in on Smiley's revenge schemes behind the scenes—along with the rest of the cast, and he had finally conceded that it was unlikely that any more movies would appear on his résumé.

To salve his wounded pride, he ramped up his stand-up appearances on the weekends and whenever *The Daily Show* went on a brief hiatus to allow staffers a vacation. Stewart discovered that the world of stand-up was a much different place for him in 2003 than even a few years earlier. For one, he filled larger venues where audiences were actually paying attention, now that he was famous. "I like going back to that now and again," he said. "I try to do a show at least once a month, just to talk about whatever's on my mind at the time."

Also bringing him back from the brink of destruction that was *Smoochy*, *Newsweek* chose Stewart for their annual "Who's Next?" prize for 2004, for which they name the celebrity most likely to make a big splash the following year.

In retrospect, the magazine was spot-on in their prediction, and not just for Stewart's professional accomplishments.

With the primaries in the spring of 2004, *The Daily Show* headed into its second full presidential campaign season, with the highlight being the 2004 Republican and Democratic National Conventions. It was clear the tide was turning: politicians were starting to realize that making an appearance on *The Daily Show* was an effective and easy way to reach America's younger voters.

The trend harkened back to earlier presidential campaigns, most notably in 1992, when Governor Bill Clinton appeared on *The Arsenio Hall Show* to serenade viewers with his saxophone. But it dates back even further to 1968, when candidate Richard M. Nixon appeared on *Rowan & Martin's Laugh-In* and told the audience to "Sock it to me," the mantra of the show.

Just before the Iowa caucuses in 2004, the campaigns for Governor Howard Dean and Senator John Kerry called *The Daily Show* producers and said they wanted to be interviewed on the show; at the time, Dean was ahead of Kerry in the polls. Stewart and Colbert loved the idea. "We'll do it like Paris Hilton and Nicole Richie on *The Simple Life*, two rich East Coast Ivy League men who try to slum on the farm to connect with the farmers," said Colbert.

When Colbert and crew showed up for the shoot, Kerry was nowhere in sight. He'd suddenly shot ahead of Dean in the polls by eight points, and instead of the campaign bus crammed full of reporters and staffers, Kerry started to travel by helicopter and forgot all about the interview. "The Dean people are in full panic mode and don't want to talk to anybody," said Colbert. They tried to make amends, and promised they'd see if Dean would be available in a few days, but Colbert would have none of it.

"We reminded them that we're fake press and are only here for two days in order to create the illusion that we're going to be here for the entire campaign," he explained. "I said if they didn't give us an interview today, there's absolutely nothing for us to put on the air. We'll shoot lock-offs of locations and do it in front of a green screen, but no interview and we're leaving at three o'clock. So, yes, we travel with the press, but only to the point where we can create the illusion that we're press. We never forget that we're not," said Colbert.

In the end, both Dean and Kerry appeared on the show, but in very different capacities and time frames. Dean appeared in a taped spoof interview with Stewart during the primary season, and Kerry appeared just before the Democratic convention. Stewart ended up on the receiving end of public backlash as the result of both.

First, the Dean sit-down was a sophomoric attempt at humor for both sides, a five-minute formal interview segment punctuated with thought-bubble asides that were poorly acted by both. But the Kerry interview put Stewart under even more scrutiny, primarily for his out-of-character softball exchange.

"It was impossible to get an interview with John Kerry at the time," said Tucker Carlson, the former host of the CNN show *Crossfire*. Once Stewart landed the interview, he disappointed many viewers. "He asked him questions like, 'Why are people so mean to you? How did you get so great? What is your vision for America?' It's a Nerf interview."

Even though he was quick to point out that he's not a journalist for perhaps the thousandth time since *The Daily Show* began, the criticism shocked Stewart. He scrutinized his own behavior and soon launched an about-face campaign of his own to resurrect his reputation. Never one to shy away from pointing fingers at the news media and politicians at large, the old version of Stewart came out, and he ramped up his attacks across the board.

Though critics and reviewers had accused Stewart of producing and hosting an ultraliberal show from the first week he took over, Stewart maintained that he was an equal opportunity comedian when it came to poking fun at the different political parties. A team of Pew researchers combed through every show aired in the second half of 2007 and found that "Stewart's humor targeted Republicans more than three times as often as Democrats. The Bush administration alone was the focus of 22 percent of the segments."

However, Pew concluded that things weren't as unbalanced as they seemed. "The fact that more jokes are made about conservatives and Republicans is largely a function that the

Republicans hold the White House and have been in power for the last seven years," observed David Hinckley, critic-at-large for the New York *Daily News*. "Bush is Christmas, Hanukah, and New Year's all rolled into one. Among comedians and satirists, Bush is a gold mine."

Colbert agrees, though he adds that Stewart cares less about the political leanings of a potential target than the intent. "Jon is admirably balanced," he said. "He pursues the true intention of the person speaking, left or right [in order] to be able to honestly mock."

"What we go after are not actual policies but the façade behind them," said Stewart. "We work in the area between the makeup they're wearing and the real face. And in that space, you can pretty much hammer away at anybody."

However, at the same time, head writer Steve Bodow was looking forward to taking the show in a new direction in 2007. "[We've enjoyed] many, many, many comedic opportunities from George Bush, but we're very glad to see him go, politically and also comedically," he said. "We've really been working with and on him for all this time, but let's get some new material and some new challenges."

And so this could be part of the reason why Stewart started to go after Kerry that same year; in 2007 the Bush presidency was in its waning days, and Stewart and his team might have to start to gear up to learn how to make fun of a Democratic president. He started to turn the tables by appearing on *Larry King Live* to criticize John Kerry. "If anyone has ever been raised in a laboratory to become president, it's Kerry," he said. "From the age of three, he got his 'My First White House' kit. Now that he's finally in the race to be president, he has decided [to be] a likable average Joe, and it so clearly goes against his constitution.

"All [politicians] run to this weird sense of 'I'm going to put on that red-and-black-check jacket and I'm going to go down to a factory and have a cup of coffee and a doughnut with a dude and show him that I'm an idiot.'"

He also quickly squashed rumors that he might enter politics himself.

Despite his about-face on Kerry, politicians continued to flock to the *Show*, equating an appearance with an instantaneous rise in visibility and name recognition among younger Americans. In the fall of 2004, John Edwards, former President Clinton, Pat Buchanan, and John McCain all appeared on the show, though Stewart's line of questioning remained a bit less confrontational with them than some would have liked.

Besides, Stewart still didn't think of himself as particularly political. "People confuse political interest with interest in current events," he pointed out. "The political industry is devoted to the electing and un-electing of officials, and that can be corrosive. If the Republicans don't lose either house, people will talk about Karl Rove's genius. There's no genius. It will be the triumph of machine and money and strategy over reality. I don't think that's anything to honor or enjoy."

The political campaign industry is also focused on manipulating the media, and Stewart reserved special vitriol for those reporters and anchors who allowed it to happen, further ramping up his well-worn attacks on the media.

"They've all become part of the same organism and no longer see themselves as the *other*," he continued. "Journalists have become stars, and their stardom is about who they can get, and by getting the right person they can keep advancing. The paradigm has switched."

He summed up his perspective this way. "There's a difference between making a point and having an agenda," Stewart said. "We don't have an agenda to change the political system. We have a more selfish agenda, to entertain ourselves. We feel a frustration with the way politics are handled and the way politics are handled within the media."

He also changed his tone about the show, softening his take a bit in a subtle way. "It's not fake news," he added. "We are not newsmen, but it's jokes about real news. We don't make anything up, other than the fact we're not actually standing in Baghdad. The appeal of doing the show is that it's cathartic."

Some may have been surprised by the change, but there may have been a good reason behind it: Stewart was now a father. Nathan Thomas Stewart was born on July 3, 2004—Jon and Tracey named him after Stewart's grandfather. Almost from the beginning they called him Little Man.

He now had the chance to prove that he was a better father than the one who had deserted him.

He barely had time to adjust to life as a new father before a series of events in the fall of 2004 raised his profile along with his workload.

In the wake of the conventions—indeed, even while they were still going on—*The Daily Show* got noticed in a big way. Even though ratings and reviews were both growing, the buzz was getting even louder: on September 19, 2004, right in the middle of the election coverage, *The Daily Show* won two Emmy

Awards for Outstanding Writing for a Variety, Music or Comedy Program as well as for Outstanding Variety, Music, or Comedy Series.

Approximately 1.1 million people viewed each episode of *The Daily Show*, an increase of 20 percent for 2004 alone. But what was even more satisfying was that the show achieved a 0.74 rating for the third quarter; *The O'Reilly Factor* was just slightly ahead at 0.76.

Best of all, in the first nine months of 2004, Comedy Central added fifty new advertisers. "*The Daily Show* is a good piece of that," said Hank Close, Comedy Central executive vice-president of advertising sales. "It's a very, very strong driver of our revenue."

"It's an advertisers' sweet spot," said Brad Adgate, senior vice-president of corporate research at Horizon Media. "Young people are the least likely to read a newspaper or watch TV news, and *The Daily Show* is one show that really has found a niche."

When some TV shows become successful, occasionally advertisers will request that the producers clamp down on including anything in the show that could be viewed as controversial or negative toward the product. While former *Daily Show* correspondent Bob Wiltfong had seen that this was often the case in his days spent in traditional TV news, he said he never saw any signs of this happening at *The Daily Show*. "The show was so successful, they didn't dare touch it," he said. "As a former TV correspondent, I felt like there was less concern about what advertisers thought while we were in the editing room or writing, and there was never any talk of whether Comedy Central would lose advertising revenue if we made this joke.

'Do we need to take off the gloves with this guy but not with that guy because of his connections with Viacom?' No, that never happened, while when I was working on a real TV news show, it did occasionally come up: 'Run this, and we'll lose this advertiser.' But never at *The Daily Show*, and I was surprised. I thought, this is the way *real* journalism should be."

However, perhaps the most surprising bit of information to come out of the studies was that though the show—and Comedy Central—was long known as an efficient way for advertisers to reach the 18–34 demographic, after the conventions ended and the election season heated up, the average viewer actually began to grow older. According to *Advertising Age*, the median age of the average *Daily Show* viewer for the third quarter of 2004 was 35.7; in comparison, the median age for news shows on the three major networks was a whopping 60-plus. The age of the average *O'Reilly* viewer was pegged at 58.

The day after the Emmy ceremonies, Jon Stewart and the writing staff from *The Daily Show* released *America (The Book): A Citizen's Guide to Democracy*, a mock high school history textbook that hit number one on *The New York Times* bestsellers list in its first week of release. While Walmart banned the book because it contained fake naked pictures of the Supreme Court justices—reimagined as cutout paper dolls—*Publishers Weekly* named it the Book of the Year.

"So much of what was out there already were polemics, books of emotional destruction," said Stewart. "The idea of this is to be the emotional opposite. What's the coldest, most analytical book you could write? A textbook! We wanted this to be an overview of the system, as opposed to a personal kick in the [balls]."

Even though the book's publication was a personal coup not only for Stewart but for the show he had built and nurtured, perhaps the most personal and heartfelt accomplishment came when he appeared on the CNN show *Crossfire* on October 15, 2004, though it was at times painful to watch his exchange with host Tucker Carlson and cohost Paul Begala.

In the years since 1999 and Stewart's debut on *The Daily Show*, whenever he appeared on other talk shows, he did it out of a sense of duty and obligation. Even though it was clear he'd rather be somewhere else, he was always a good guest and never ruffled any feathers. So Carlson and Begala expected nothing different despite the fact that Stewart occasionally raked the show across the coals on *The Daily Show*.

What had escaped everybody's notice was that Stewart planned to do the same on their show.

When Stewart agreed to appear on the show, coming on the heels of the publication of his new book, everyone from the producers on down thought it would be a nice easy visit. Some lighthearted jabs would undoubtedly ensue, but at the end of the fourteen-minute segment, everyone would grin, shake hands, exchange a few gracious words for the sake of the audience, and then go their merry way.

But that's not what happened at all. The first person to have a clue was Begala, who met with Stewart in the green room before the show for some chitchat. He thought that Stewart's demeanor seemed off in some regard.

He later realized that Stewart had planned to go on the offensive from the very beginning, and in fact it was the reason why he agreed to appear on the show in the first place. "I thought he was going to push his book that had just come out, but he wanted to be more serious," Begala remembered.

From the beginning, Stewart was out of character and unusually humorless; he didn't smile once when speaking with Carlson. During his diatribe, he pushed his overall philosophy that claimed politicians and media are bad, and attacked both sides while saying that *Crossfire* was "hurting America."

The main sticking point of the show was when Carlson accused Stewart of playing softball with Kerry on *The Daily Show*, the same sin Stewart was hurling at Carlson on *Crossfire*. "You have him on your show and you sniff his throne and you are accusing us of partisan hackery?" asked an incredulous Carlson.

"Absolutely," Stewart replied.

Carlson: "You have got to be kidding me!"

"You are on CNN," said Stewart, "the show that leads into me is puppets making crank phone calls. What is wrong with you?"

After several more volleys exchanged between Stewart and the cohosts, Carlson whined, "I thought you were going to be funny."

"No," said Stewart, "I'm not going to be your monkey."

Later on, Carlson reflected on the segment. "I knew he had these kinds of pretensions about being a political thinker, but I didn't take him seriously and I don't take him seriously now," he said. "I was shocked by the preachiness of it, and was kind of embarrassed for him."

Whatever Carlson thought, the exchange attracted the attention of viewers, critics, and CNN.

"When Stewart snapped at Tucker that way, it was one of those flash points in television," said David Hinckley. "We've got this era now when reality TV means anything *but* reality, so you get a moment like *that* on *Crossfire* and think, *whoa*. It's like you've been slapped in the face. This was real."

However, other critics weren't buying Stewart's defense. "The puppet thing is just his way of deflecting," said Rachel Sklar, lawyer and former editor at *The Huffington Post*. "The fact is that *The Daily Show* and *The Colbert Report* are more than just shows that go on at eleven o'clock at night to a specific number of viewers. They're picked up the next day on YouTube. They're picked up by blogs. And they're picked up as . . . genuine news stories on the Associated Press."

Sklar wasn't done. "He's a good interviewer and he knows his stuff. And when people are on the show, they have genuine discussions, and sometimes they break news."

Looking back, it's not like the *Crossfire* host hadn't been warned. In the weeks leading up to his *Crossfire* appearance, Stewart had appeared on several shows—including National Public Radio's *Fresh Air*—touting the same ideas as a warm-up.

"Political parties are basically dedicated to figuring out how to game the system . . . and are actively exploiting that loophole," he told host Terry Gross.

And his criticisms had existed years before, when Stewart characterized the tone of his show just a week into his tenure back in 1999: "*The Daily Show* seems to be a nice sort of pin in the balloon," he said.

Crossfire had expected him to be the typical convivial, slightly smirking talk-show host always ready with a quick retort or arch comment or observation to poke fun at someone in the news. But he'd shown up with a more serious agenda. In any case, while the highly charged exchange brought out the critics in some corners, it only served to cement Stewart as a hero in others.

Stewart had only two regrets about his appearance. "The reason everyone on *Crossfire* freaked out is that I didn't play the role I was supposed to play. I was expected to do some funny jokes, then go have a beer with everyone." He also noted that some critics thought he had a personal beef with Carlson because of the caustic back and forth between them, but Stewart maintains he was specifically criticizing the tone and format of the show and not the hosts.

What happened next surprised even Stewart: *Crossfire* was canceled shortly after his appearance. Jonathan Klein, the recently hired president of CNN, succumbed to pressure from advertisers—which was nonexistent before Stewart went on the show, though the show had also experienced lower ratings over the previous year—and announced that he'd cancel the show. "I guess I come down more firmly in the Jon Stewart camp," he said. "I doubt that when the president sits down with his advisers they scream at him to bring him up to date on all of the issues. I don't know why we don't treat the audience with the same respect."

In the wake of *Crossfire*, however, some other members of the media were beginning to publicly take issue with Stewart's constant finger-pointing and his harangues directed toward them and their supposed lack of integrity.

"The Jon Stewart backlash should start right about now," said Wonkette founder Ana Marie Cox after news of the cancellation hit. "Stewart has pretty much painted a target on his chest with his *Crossfire* appearance. To say his is just a comedy show is a cop-out in a way. He's gotten so much power. So many people look to him that you can't really be the kid in the back throwing spitballs."

"Jon gets to decide the rules governing his own activism and the causes he supports and how often he does it," said Brian Williams, anchor of the *NBC Nightly News*. "And his audience gets to decide if they like the serious Jon as much as they do the satirical Jon.

"He has chronicled the death of shame in politics and journalism, and many of us on this side of the journalism tracks often wish we were on Jon's side," Williams added. "I envy his platform to shout from the mountaintop. He's a necessary branch of government."

Veteran newsman Ted Koppel also stepped into the fray. "Jon feels [journalists] should be more opinionated, not less, and he feels I have a responsibility to get in there and tell the public, 'Look, this guy is lying'—although maybe not quite that blatantly," he said. "I disagree with that only in part. In a live interview you can say, 'That doesn't sound right,' but you don't automatically have all the facts at your disposal. Jon is really profoundly concerned and angry about real issues, but a satirist gets to poke and prod and make fun of other people, and when you say, 'What about you, dummy?' he says, 'I'm just a satirist.'"

For Stewart's part, at this stage in his life, all the criticism just tended to roll off his back. "I really feel like I have gotten to this weird place where rejection is a good kind of pain," he said. "Like you get a shot to the ribs sometimes and you go, eh, I'm alive, you know what I mean? Like you get to a certain baseline where you feel confident in your ability to do that tiny little thing that you do. And the other stuff that you've been allowed to do is sort of gravy, and if it doesn't work out, that's really all right."

Some serious journalists continued to cheer him on. "Jon Stewart doesn't claim to be a journalist, and when he says he's not we should believe it," said Robert Thompson, director of the Bleier Center for Television and Popular Culture at Syracuse University. "His interviews are in the tradition of Johnny Carson, where he's polite, at times deferential, and behaves in the interviews like a well-brought-up young man." In Thompson's view, that's where they part company and Stewart morphs into something totally unique. "When all the news guys were walking on eggshells [during the Iraq war], Jon was hammering those questions about WMDs. That's the kind of thing CNN and CBS should have been doing."

Even the formidable Bill Moyers, a veteran newsman who served as press secretary to President Lyndon B. Johnson before launching a decades-long career in political journalism in network news and public broadcasting, weighed in with effusive praise that was unusual for him. "When I report the news on this broadcast, people say I'm making it up, but when Stewart makes it up, they say he's telling the truth," said Moyers. "When future historians come to write the political story of our times, they will first have to review hundreds of hours of a cable television program called *The Daily Show*. You simply can't understand American politics in the new millennium without *The Daily Show*."

. . .

As the presidential campaign of 2004 ran on, the lines between real and fake news continued to blur in Stewart's world,
as well as on the show.

First, John Edwards went on the show to announce his
presidential candidacy. Stewart quipped, "We are a fake show,
so you might have to do this again somewhere."

Then Stewart announced that he planned to vote for John
Kerry. While it wasn't a total surprise given that the most frequent targets on the show happen to be Republicans, the fact that
he aired it in public made it appear to be an endorsement coming
from not only him but the show, which was an unusual move.

"There's no question that at a certain point that we were
leaning toward a certain election result," he said. "That doesn't
mean we thought one side was pure and the other evil. If you
watched this show and didn't know I was voting for Kerry
you're clearly not paying attention to the show. But if you
think that by announcing it that I've lost my credibility as a
comedian, I just didn't think we had any credibility to lose."

Even though he continually maintained that he had no
power, it was crystal clear that he wished to have an impact on
the business-as-usual politics and the media. However, to his
great dismay, both just dug in their heels and became more
entrenched, sensationalistic, and polarized. On the show the
night before the 2004 presidential election, he had this to say:

"Tomorrow when you go to the polls, make my life difficult. Make the next four years *really* hard, so that every morning all we can do is come in and go, 'Madonna is doing some
kabbalah thing, you wanna do that?' I'd like that. I'm tired."

Perhaps as the result of the combination of all of these
things, an interesting thing happened: Stewart was no longer

the funniest guy on the show, the clown. He morphed from the zany one on the show and turned into the calm one, the occasionally austere older anchor while all around him the—mostly younger—correspondents acted out of turn, went for the cheap joke or visual or pratfall. Though he may deny he is anything but a comedian until the day he dies, Stewart had turned into an authority figure along the way.

The Daily Show had made a star out of its host, and now the same thing was starting to happen with its correspondents.

After the success of his costarring role as Evan Baxter in the 2003 Jim Carrey movie *Bruce Almighty*, Steve Carell was already getting more movie and TV offers from Hollywood. He left *The Daily Show* in the spring of 2004 to begin work on the American version of *The Office*, based on a popular BBC series, and *The 40-Year-Old Virgin*, a movie that would be released in 2005. After Carell's departure, Colbert became the next in line, but it was clear that Stewart wasn't going anywhere soon.

However, in addition to his hosting and producing duties, Stewart was actively searching for new projects for his Busboy Productions to take on. He had recently signed a deal with Comedy Central to pursue new projects, and they didn't have to look far.

And then just like that, it was Colbert's turn.

"At that time, he was a total rock star among correspondents," said Bob Wiltfong. "When any of his stories ran, there was a huge reaction from the audience. The feeling among the rest of us was, why is this guy still on the show?"

Besides, Colbert was getting restless. "I couldn't imagine how much longer I could do it," he said. "I still liked it, and I didn't want to *not* like it."

"If your name's not Jon Stewart, there's only so many places you can go on *The Daily Show*," said executive producer Ben Karlin. "Steve Carell and Steve Colbert were the first two we identified as giant talents with breakout potential, but we didn't have the mechanism in place when Steve Carell started getting offers, so he left. With Stephen, we didn't want to have him go off and become a huge star without working with him."

"He'd been there a long time," added Karlin. "He was never going to be the host, it was Jon's show. But we didn't want to lose him, so we tried to figure out what else someone like Stephen could do."

They remembered those fake promos for the fake *Colbert Report* that had aired several times on *The Daily Show*. One day in the fall of 2003, when working on scripts for *The Daily Show*, the producers and writers had discovered that one segment was running a bit short.

Why not run a fake ad for a fake show starring a fake news correspondent?

They ran it by Colbert, and it sounded good to him. The writers came up with a promo for the imaginary *Colbert Report* despite the fact that the show didn't exist.

"I tried to ape whoever was the loudest and rightest in prime-time cable news," he said. They produced four of these promos, which ran through 2003 and 2004, and thought nothing more of it.

Executives at Comedy Central were looking to extend *The Daily Show* franchise, as were Stewart and Karlin for Busboy Productions. Perhaps the fake promos had planted the seed, but building a show around Colbert's character seemed doable.

The O'Reilly Factor with Stephen Colbert was how they pitched it.

Once they started to flesh out the show, Colbert said, "But I can't be an asshole."

"You're not an asshole," said Stewart. "You're an idiot. There's a difference."

Colbert agreed. "The audience wouldn't forgive Jon for saying things most comedians would want to say," he said. "But we can say almost anything, because it's coming out of the mouth of this character."

"The challenge of these things is how to evolve and keep it fresh and keep people from being bored with your voice," said Stewart. "We were lucky to have the guy as long as we had him. In fact, one year we kept him because we hid his keys."

The deal was made and announced in the spring of 2005: Stephen Colbert would host his own show starting in the fall. And Stewart's Busboy Productions would serve as executive producers.

The first episode of *The Colbert Report* went on the air on October 17, 2005.

"It became so clear so quickly that it was going to work that it was kind of astounding," said Comedy Central president Doug Herzog. "When the show debuted, I remember thinking that it had been birthed fully baked. That's so rare. I don't know if I've ever seen it before. The whole thing fits him like a glove. It's really a virtuoso performance."

"*The Colbert Report* depends on Stephen's ability to process information as this other person," said Stewart. "Watch Colbert and it's like the first time you use broadband: 'How the fuck did that happen?' He's rendering in real time. He's basically doing his show in a second language."

After only eight shows, Comedy Central renewed *The Colbert Report* for an entire year.

For all of the critiquing and finger-pointing he was doing at the media and politicians, it turned out that in his private life—which he still heavily guarded—Stewart was turning into one big softy.

"When I look at Nathan, I think, I could kill someone for him. In fact, I could do it almost every day," he admitted.

"I am a neutered cat, which is a very contented and warm feeling."

CHAPTER 10

IN THE SPRING of 2006, Stewart got his chance to perform in the ultimate stand-up venue:

The Oscars.

It was a controversial choice. For the most part, the celebrities chosen to host the annual awards ceremony are reliable middle-of-the-road stars, like Billy Crystal and Johnny Carson. In other words, stars who were considered safe, not automatically detested by a good chunk of the American public, and who wouldn't run off the rails in front of an audience of up to 55 million people—the audience for the 1998 show when the movie *Titanic* attracted a record audience. Chris Rock had hosted the 2005 show, and viewership for the night had dropped 3 percent from the year before, going from 43.5 million viewers in 2004 to 42.1 million in 2005.

The Oscar producers also didn't like the potential for political humor to disrupt the flow of the night—or for a host to unleash a few barbed zingers—and so the selection of Stewart was definitely a risk because they wanted to draw in more young viewers.

Stewart and his wife, Tracey McShane, attending the Governor's Ball at the Academy Awards on March 5, 2006. *(Courtesy BEImages/Alex J. Berliner)*

"You have to be humorous and able to prick the pomposity of it without coming across as mean-spirited or nasty," said Damien Bona, author of *Inside Oscar.*

"It's a lot of pressure; I'm very glad I'm not getting ready right now," Chris Rock said in advance of the 2006 broadcast. "This time last year, I was losing my mind."

For his part, Stewart tried to distract himself from the task at hand. "Free time is death to the anxious, and thank goodness I don't have any of it right now," he said.

Stewart fully realized the precarious situation he was in—as well as acknowledging the real honor—and so for the most part he played it safe. The most political joke he told was this: "I do have some sad news to report: Björk couldn't be here tonight. She was trying on her Oscar dress and Dick Cheney shot her."

The rest of the time, he stuck to the tried-and-true with quips like, "We've got movies about racism, prejudice, censorship, murders. This is why we go to movies, for an escape," and "The Oscars is really I guess the one night of the year when you can see all your favorite stars without having to donate any money to the Democratic Party. And it's exciting for the stars as well because it's the first time many of you have ever voted for a winner."

The critics were not kind. "It's hard to believe that professional entertainers could have put together a show less entertaining than this year's Oscars, hosted with a smug humorlessness by comic Jon Stewart, a sad and pale shadow of great hosts gone by," said Tom Shales of the *Washington Post*.

The *New York Times* hurled the biggest insult anyone could at Stewart: "He wasn't as funny as he usually is," wrote the critic.

"He's such a great performer and that's what makes it so hard," said his mentor, Caroline Hirsch. "That audience is an audience of performers, and it's almost like they're saying, prove it to me, make me laugh. And that's hard to do. Doing the Oscars is a really hard gig."

To be sure, the show didn't get off to a great start. "The show began with a montage of previous hosts turning down the thankless gig, making Stewart seem like the last guy standing after a game of musical chairs," wrote Gary Susman, a critic with Moviefone.com.

In his own postmortem, Stewart didn't beat himself up over the reviews. "When you're dealing with a group where eighty percent are walking home empty-handed, you want to make sure that when that night is over they don't feel like they have just wasted twelve hours," he said. "I actually didn't think it was such a bad job."

However, in the wake of the Oscars, some critics—and viewers—began to think that now that he was in his eighth year of meeting the grinding demands of *The Daily Show*, maybe it was time for Stewart to take a break, maybe look to something different and let someone else take the reins for a while.

Executive producer Ben Karlin—in many eyes, Stewart's anchor since day one—had been essentially running both shows since he assumed responsibility for the launch of *The Colbert Report* in 2005, and he had finally confessed he was wrung out from the schedule in 2006.

Plus, maybe the bigger sin was that after almost eight years of full-tilt production, it was simply a lot harder to come up with something funny. "You definitely get more intellectual about comedy," Karlin admitted. "The laugh impulse has been deadened."

Part of the problem was that *The Daily Show* was tried-and-true, while *The Colbert Report* was fresh and new, and though it was still finding its legs, the format and tone were so radically different from Stewart's show that viewers increasingly opted to watch Colbert over Stewart.

One critic hit the nail on the head when he suggested the reason why *The Daily Show* was starting to feel like a chore. "*The Daily Show* is like a really good marriage: solid, dependable, and deeply satisfying, but the mystery, wonder, and freshness are gone. I still think *The Daily Show* suffers from the absence of a Colbert or Carell. *The Colbert Report*, on the other hand, is like the giddy infatuation of new love. Anything seems possible. The sky's the limit."

And so while viewers who were inclined to watch both shows back-to-back may have had Stewart's show on as background, as soon as 11:30 hit, they turned up the volume on the TV and really focused on Colbert. At that point, you never knew what he would do or say. The novelty of watching him introduce a guest and then run around the studio waving and bowing and accepting the audience's raucous applause was still fresh. Plus, the caliber of guests he was able to attract was already leagues beyond Stewart's: one night, Stewart interviewed Ben Stiller, while Colbert spoke with Peter Frampton and Henry Kissinger, both interviewed in his inimitable razor-sharp style.

"The jokes in each episode of *The Daily Show* now follow a rigid pattern," wrote another critic. "Either they show a clip of a politician saying something stupid, followed by a cut to Stewart's shocked/bemused expression, or Stewart has to deal with a fake news 'correspondent' who doesn't quite understand what is going on in the world. While *The Colbert Report* could be weird to the point of incomprehensibility, it was at least surprising."

Perhaps it was inevitable, but another problem with the *Show* was that Stewart's particular brand of satirical fake news had begun to spread as traditional news programs started to ride Stewart's coattails and began to adopt some of *The Daily Show*'s characteristics. Keith Olbermann, who helped launch the MS-NBC show *Countdown* in 2003, introduced a couple of segments in 2005 and 2006—respectively Worst Person in the World and Special Comments—which could have been lifted directly from a Stewart monologue, often poking fun and criticizing George W. Bush and Fox News. Soon, other news hosts and programs followed suit in both national and smaller markets.

Stewart was also picking some odd fights, and in a very public way. When he hosted financial expert Jim Cramer, host of CNBC's *Mad Money*, on the show in the spring of 2009, both Comedy Central and CNBC played it up for the week preceding as being the fight of the century, or at least a good rollicking repeat of Stewart's *Crossfire* appearance.

Essentially, Stewart accused Cramer and his network of complicity for misleading his viewers with inaccurate and over-the-top financial advice in the period before the economy began to tank in 2008.

"I understand that you want to make finance entertaining, but it's not a fucking game," said Stewart. "We're both snake-oil salesmen to a certain extent. But we do label the show as snake oil here. Isn't there a problem selling snake oil as vitamin tonic and saying that it cures impetigo?"

Instead of fighting back like Tucker Carlson had done, however, Cramer meekly nodded and agreed with Stewart's barbs for the most part. "I try really hard to make as many good calls as I can," he said. "I, too, like you, want to have a successful show. Should we have been constantly pointing out the mistakes that were made? Absolutely. I truly wish we had done more."

While some critics—and many financial advisers—applauded Stewart for taking on Cramer, others had had enough of his good-guy tactics.

Regular fans were beginning to turn away. "Typically, I am a fan of *The Daily Show*, but I honestly believe Jon Stewart has taken a low blow with this verbal scuffle with Jim Cramer," said one viewer. "Not only is it mean-spirited and unnecessary, but it's not funny. And just as Cramer is paid to excite us about Wall Street, Stewart is paid to make us laugh. I wish he'd get back to work."

Was Stewart getting tired? Was he getting so restless that he could no longer hide it? After all, it had been a decade since he had taken over from Craig Kilborn, who himself succumbed to complacency and predictability in the rigors of creating a new show from scratch four nights a week and had left *The Late Late Show with Craig Kilborn* just five years after ditching *The Daily Show*.

Though Stewart has never outwardly admitted if he's been blocked—whether by a lack of creativity or by sheer exhaustion—he has said that the pressure of an insane deadline never fails to spur him on to finding just the right joke or new angle for a sketch.

Or maybe it was just the simple fact that he was so happy and content in his personal life that the pressure and crushing deadlines that he had to endure at the studio on a daily basis were getting harder to take. "When I'm in, I'm in," he said.

He also had just become a father for the second time. Daughter Maggie Rose Stewart was born in February 2006, and though he had adjusted nicely to life with his son, he was a bit nervous about the prospect of dealing with a daughter.

"I don't know that much about women," he said. "A boy child, I feel like I'll know how to deal with it if he has a problem. I'll just be able to say to him, 'Well, repress it,' and hopefully he'll swallow that, as I have. And then you figure you have thirty years before it comes out over dinner where somebody spills the gravy and then you're like 'I hate you!'

"But a girl, she's going to want me to have tea with her and her panda. What am I going to do with that?"

To accommodate his growing family, in 2005 he and Tracey had bought a six-thousand-square-foot Tribeca duplex penthouse loft for almost $6 million through a real estate trust named the Shamsky Monkey Trust after his cat and dog. A few years later in 2008, *Forbes* would estimate his annual income at $14 million.

The loft quickly became his retreat from the world, and after the postmortem on the show wraps, he rushes out the door and heads downtown for home to see his wife and kids and animals. Most surprisingly, he turns into the polar opposite of his TV persona once he closes the door behind him. "He never talks about politics or world events," Tracey said.

His sense of humor also morphs into something entirely different. "He's silly, but it's not like I live with a jokester," she added. "He's not annoying and not always on. Jon is not even that smart at home. He's really all about his family."

His dogs now included a new third addition, a three-legged pooch named Little Dipper. "The whole family can fit in one bed with three dogs placed strategically," he said. "And the dogs are all pretty good about going under the covers and curling up. One nice thing is that it does generate a lot of heat. It's like having one of those brick ovens that they make pizza in. The three of them get in there and it fires us up to thermonuclear levels."

Both Tracey and Jon were totally enthralled with being parents. "We both think the same things are funny and we both value the same things. So parenting for us is very easy as far as our relationship goes because we always see eye to eye [with] the kids," said Tracey. "Nate is very gentle, sweet, sensi-

Stewart takes his three-legged dog, Champ, for a walk in New York in spring 2013. *(Courtesy FameFlynet Pictures)*

tive, emotional, and kind and loves *Star Wars* and football, while Maggie is hilarious and irreverent, like her dad in girl form. . . . I always say that she's me on the inside and Jon on the outside. And Nate is Jon on the outside and me on the inside."

Unlike many celebrities and people in the public eye, Stewart purposely avoids the spotlight. "I'm not a particularly social animal," he said. Indeed, he rarely attends black-tie events in Manhattan and once even passed up the chance to pick up an Emmy at the annual awards ceremony. "You go to a party, those people don't need you to open shit or help them get their pants on. So they're not nearly so nice to you."

One of the Stewart family's favorite things to do is to watch the Food Network, particularly *Restaurant Impossible*, *Cupcake Wars*, *Chopped*, and *Iron Chef*. Though Tracey doesn't like to cook, the food shows have motivated both Nate and Maggie to learn to cook.

While Stewart's outlook and priorities were changing and he seemed understandably exhausted, he may have become less funny than he used to be for another reason: when he first started hosting the *Show* back in 1999, Stewart still expected that his efforts would bring about some kind of change in the world, particularly the divisive, bitter world of American politics. Maybe it was a bit unrealistic, but he had held out hope that he could make a difference. While he still felt that way, it had become clear he had to shift gears and take real action in order to put his beliefs to the test.

So on December 16, 2010, Stewart devoted the entire *Daily Show* to the fact that thousands of September 11 first responders were suffering from some serious health problems. Even though Congress had crafted a bill that would give firefighters, policemen and -women, and EMTs a wide range of benefits to help them deal with it, a Republican filibuster late in the session—and before their lengthy vacation—stalled the bill, making it unlikely to pass. He also predictably chided the news media for not calling attention to the issue.

Stewart and his producers put their heads together and handpicked a roundtable of first responders to appear on a panel to tell their stories. A few days later, Congress ferried the bill through a vote and passed it. The local firemen were so thrilled that they threw a birthday party for Stewart's daughter at the firehouse—complete with a fire truck–shaped birthday cake—and Robert J. Thompson, a professor at Syracuse University, instantly vaulted him to having the same status and influence as both Walter Cronkite and Edward R. Murrow, veteran newsmen who used their influence to turn around, respectively, a war and a government witch hunt.

Even though Stewart emphatically maintained time and again that he was *not* a journalist, a 2007 Pew survey showed that Americans believed Stewart to be on a par with Dan Rather and Tom Brokaw as the most widely admired journalists in the United States. Indeed, upon Cronkite's death in 2009, *Time* magazine conducted a poll to ask readers their suggestions for his replacement as "most trusted man in America." Stewart won with 44 percent of the vote, but predictably downplayed the results.

Despite the feeling of satisfaction Stewart derived from these accomplishments, it was just getting too difficult to bring about the kind of significant change that he hoped for. And there weren't enough *Daily Show* episodes in the course of a year to change everything that he felt needed correcting on the political front.

Some missteps were beginning to appear along the way. On a 2009 *Daily Show*, out of nowhere Stewart told the audience he believed that President Harry Truman should have been considered a war criminal when he dropped atomic bombs on Hiroshima and Nagasaki. Overnight, widespread outrage predictably ensued from all political and social fronts, and Stewart came out with a public apology on the show a couple of days later:

"Right after saying it, I thought to myself: that was dumb," he admitted. "And it *was* dumb. Stupid, in fact. So I shouldn't have said that, and I say right now, no, I don't believe that to be the case."

Stewart won kudos from some unexpected fronts, with

many conservatives saying he was right the first time. "I was a bit surprised, albeit pleasantly, to see Jon Stewart nail Harry Truman as a war criminal," opined conservative critic Justin Raimondo, suggesting that it was Comedy Central executives who forced Stewart's apology, and not his fans. After all, the audience that day actually cheered at Stewart's announcement during the show.

"Rule number one in this game is that everybody must play their assigned role," Raimondo continued, "you've always got to be 'in character.' If you're on the left, you can take on George W. Bush, murderer of hundreds of thousands of Iraqis—but not Harry Truman, killer of even larger numbers of innocent Japanese civilians."

Karlin also attempted a feeble save on account of his boss. "Oftentimes, people who say satiric or unpleasant things are labeled as curmudgeons," he said. "Jon has a very rare gift for being able to deliver material that has bite, but not in a mean or nasty way."

But not everyone agreed, including a fellow comedian who had good reason to be eternally grateful to Stewart for providing his springboard to stardom. "It's one thing poking fun at people who deserve it," said Steve Carell. "But there was [always] that flip side of shooting fish in a barrel. It's just cruel."

And even one of his oldest friends, Anthony Weiner, turned on him. "I think that [cynicism] exists because of Jon's show," he said. "I think it becomes a feedback loop that's corrosive. Congressmen do dumb things, then they're highlighted for doing dumb things, and people watch it and say that congressmen do dumb things, and so then when another congressman does a dumb thing, [Stewart says], 'Well, my audience wants to watch a congressman do a dumb thing.' So when the audience laughs at the congressman doing a dumb thing, Jon says, 'Hey, I got a great scam here, lemme go find another congressman doing a dumb thing.'"

It almost looked like Stewart was starting to realize the futility of his efforts to change politics and its media, where he was tempted to just say "fuck it" and succumb to his hermitlike tendencies. Especially when dealing with people who should know better, like the hosts of national talk shows.

Stewart launched into a diatribe on *Larry King Live* about the totally artificial front that politicians present to the public, and that they rarely reveal their true selves. "When you get a glimpse behind the façade that they put up, they're completely different people," he ranted. "We should stop pretending that they're not and they should stop pretending that they are these paragons of virtue and beacons of decency."

King's response: "So are you saying that all politicians hide themselves from us, their real selves? Is that what you're saying?"

Stewart's silence was followed by a heavy sigh before he finally spoke. "Please tell me you didn't just ask me that."

Not only were politicians and presidential candidates clamoring to appear on *The Daily Show*, leaders of other countries wanted to get their shot with Stewart as well.

In September of 2006, Pervez Musharraf, the president of Pakistan, was booked on the show to promote his new book *In the Line of Fire*.

"Where's Osama bin Laden?" Stewart asked him suddenly.

"I don't know," replied Musharraf. "You know where he is? You lead on, we'll follow you."

In a variation on the theme of his interview with Kerry, Stewart took a more lighthearted approach to his talk with Musharraf. After serving up tea and Twinkies, Stewart put the Pakistani president on the "Seat of Heat," a recently introduced segment where the lights go down low while a series of red lights flashed on and off before he asks his guest one last question.

"George W. Bush and Osama bin Laden—be truthful—who would win a popular vote in Pakistan?" asked Stewart.

"I think they'd both lose miserably," said Musharraf.

In the background of the usual breakneck schedule and performance in front of the camera, however, there was real trouble brewing. In late 2007, no one knew if *The Daily Show* would still be on the air in the near future, since the contract between the Writers Guild of America and TV producers and studios was set to expire. Since all *Daily Show* writers were now members of the union as of 2006, this meant that in case of a strike, there would be no show. Negotiations were ongoing, but chances for a resolution appeared to dim, and writers had already voted to strike if their demands were not met.

The main sticking points revolved around digital media royalties—including the Internet and smartphone applications—and higher payments to writers for each DVD that sold with their work in it. At the time, writers earned four cents a DVD, which they wanted to be increased to eight cents.

But like other daily news shows, even though it was a fake news show, *The Daily Show* still needed new content for each show. While some segments and features could be prepared in advance, much of the show was still cranked out up to the very last minute before taping that evening's show.

"We'll be affected by a strike, as will be everybody else," said Tony Fox, a spokesman for Comedy Central. "The two shows that are most impacted are *The Daily Show* and *The Colbert Report* because they air four nights a week."

Reruns were the only option, even though ratings plummeted whenever *The Daily Show* went into repeats. Another issue was that Stewart was a member of the Writers Guild as was Colbert. "They both write for their shows under the Writers Guild contract," said Michael Winship, president of the Writers Guild's East division. "Our position is that they could not do any of the work that they normally do as a Writers Guild member in terms of writing and performing material on the show."

As expected, talks broke down. More than twelve thousand TV, movie, and radio writers across the country went on strike on November 5, 2007, and *The Daily Show* went into repeats.

Stewart took the strike as his first chance to take a break in years, and reveled in it, though it did take a little getting used to. Other late-night shows also went into reruns, including *Late Night with Conan O'Brien*, *Late Show with David Letterman*, and *The Tonight Show with Jay Leno*.

However, pressure soon began to build from the networks that were losing money. Carson Daly was the first late-night talk-show host to return to the air, albeit reluctantly. "An ultimatum was put in front of me," said Daly. "It was, 'Put a new show on by December third or seventy-five people are fired. What's your answer?'"

Soon, other late-night shows began to cave. The next shows

to return to work—without their writers—were *Late Show with David Letterman* and *The Late Late Show with Craig Ferguson*, both on CBS. Like Daly, both hosts explained that the entire nonwriting staff would be laid off if they continued to stay off the air. In late December, these shows and *Late Night with Conan O'Brien* announced they would return to the airwaves on January 2, 2008.

Then, shortly before Christmas, Stewart announced that *The Daily Show* would return to Comedy Central on January 7th, presumably for similar reasons. He and Colbert offered up a joint statement: "We would like to return to work with our writers. If we cannot, we would like to express our ambivalence, but without our writers we are unable to express something as nuanced as ambivalence."

In acknowledgment of the striking writers, however, both Colbert and Stewart slightly altered the names of their shows: they became *A Daily Show with Jon Stewart*, while Colbert merely started pronouncing the *t*'s at the end of *Colbert* and *Report*.

It was unclear how the show would turn out, given that the writers were such a vital part of the process. But after it aired, one critic weighed in, saying he thought a writer-less *Daily Show* was an improvement:

"I found *A Daily Show* more compelling this evening," said Thomas Tennant, who covers talk shows for About.com. "Stewart focused exclusively on the New Hampshire primaries. It was wonderfully insightful and biting, maybe a bit more biting than usual. I'm going to guess his writers pull him back from the edge from time to time—or at least balance him a bit."

The *Show* struggled along for almost six more weeks without the writers, with Stewart making lots of hits and misses and off-the-cuff improvisation. Correspondent John Oliver appeared in more segments than usual because as a British citizen, he was at risk of being deported if he went on strike. On February 12, the strike officially ended, the show returned the next day, and it didn't take long for things to return to normal.

But Stewart's version of normal for years had been a cycle of sheer exhaustion when it came to the show. He had hosted *The Daily Show* for ten years now. The cracks were beginning to show. And it was clear he was looking for a new challenge.

But gripe as he might, Stewart still got fired up when he felt indignant about something, or saw someone in the middle getting stomped on.

"If I wasn't doing this, I'd be shouting at the TV," he said. "There are mornings I walk in and view the news clips and it is the opposite of turning a light on. But then we go through . . . the day and it is cathartic and energizing."

Then, after a year when Ellen DeGeneres hosted, the Academy Awards decided to give him a second chance at hosting at the 2008 ceremony.

Though his 2006 appearance had been middling, perhaps producers accepted that it wasn't the easiest job in the world. As critic Gary Susman put it, "The job requires a difficult and rare set of skills: a host must entertain both the Hollywood big shots in the auditorium and regular folks at home." He explained, "They can poke fun at the huge egos in the room, but can't deflate them with too much snark, and they can't be too inside baseball. Most of all, they have to think quickly on their feet, since there's no telling what will happen during a live show broadcast to hundreds of millions around the world."

The second time was the charm for Stewart, in part due to the types of movies that were up for multiple nominations that year, including *No Country for Old Men* and *There Will Be Blood.* "His edginess fit the tone of the material," said Susman.

With the writers' strike over and the Oscars behind him, Stewart settled into his third presidential campaign at *The Daily Show.* And what a gold mine of material it was, between the nomination of Sarah Palin as John McCain's running mate and the Democratic primary showdown between the potential first woman and first African-American president, Hillary Clinton and Barack Obama. Despite his perceived burnout, it was clear that Stewart was energized by the comic opportunities presented during the yearlong Indecision 2008.

Stewart and Colbert—along with correspondents from *The Daily Show*—joined forces on election night to present a live broadcast just as they had done in 2000 and 2004. In addition to the election of the first African-American president, another historic first occurred on the set of *The Daily Show* that very same night.

The two fake news anchors reported real news for the very first time.

The hour-long show was filled with correspondents reporting stories in front of green screens that made it seem like they were at the various campaign headquarters, but mixed in were factual updates on percentages and reports on states that had declared a clear winner. They were supposed to sign off at 11 P.M., because no one thought the election would be confirmed that night, but then one of the producers saw that CNN was going to call the election for Obama.

So they kept the cameras rolling. Rob Kutner, a *Daily Show* writer, set the scene:

"It's a few minutes after eleven. The *Colbert* writers have occupied our writers' lounge and are stinking drunk on Crystal Head Vodka," he said. "We stall it just a little longer. The producer signals to Jon and Stephen at the desk, giving them the thumbs-up. Then, Jon made the announcement, for the first time ever, delivering a piece of real news."

"I would just like to say, if I may," Stewart said, his voice catching slightly, "that at eleven o'clock at night, Eastern Standard Time, the president of the United States is Barack Obama. We don't normally do this live. We're a fake news show."

Though Colbert whooped it up during the show when a state was announced for McCain and despondently groaned when one went for Obama, when it was all over, he actually felt a bit uncomfortable. "I've never had this feeling before," he said. "Things actually went well on election night. I'm a little stunned. I don't know what to do with my happiness. I'm still afraid someone's going to take it away."

CHAPTER 11

WITH THE ELECTION of the first African-American president, viewers and critics alike expected Stewart to go easy on Obama. And indeed, Stewart did run a number of lighthearted segments on the new president in the first year, including a piece called "Obama Kills a Fly," about the moment when the president smacked a fly dead in the middle of an interview on CNBC.

Critics who predicted Stewart would soften in the wake of a new Democratic president—and who missed the Stewart of the Bush era—were rightfully disappointed in what they viewed as a toothless new version of *The Daily Show*. They might have been on track with their accusations. However, Stewart pointed out a whole other set of challenges that he and the show's producers faced after more than a decade at the helm.

For one, the speed with which a news story hits and then vanishes had ramped up several times since 1999.

And he publicly admitted that it was becoming more difficult to shake things up and make a story—and his style of approaching it—sound totally fresh and new. "I have a small bag of tricks, and try to deploy them in various permutations," he said. "Then again, I also feel that limitations are one of the keys to creativity. If it came easy, maybe I wouldn't have worked as hard."

At the same time, Stewart felt that the show had improved through the years. "I think it's a better show now than it was ten years ago, we're more consistent," he said.

With a surefire punching bag no longer occupying the White House, Stewart had to find different targets, which of course didn't take him long. But he was mystified when some not only didn't play along but fired back at him.

For instance, while Stewart never made any effort to hide his dislike of CNN even years after his *Crossfire* appearance—"Oh, I'm sorry—are we on CNN right now? I thought this was the pre-show banter," he said during an appearance on *Larry King Live* in October 2010—he continued to goad certain people for reasons that turned out to be surprising.

For example, Stewart put CNN anchor Rick Sanchez in the *Daily Show* crosshairs so often that many thought it suspicious. After Stewart had poked fun at Sanchez—who is Cuban-American—for everything from his unfamiliarity with United States geography to volunteering to be Tasered for a news story, Sanchez finally reached the breaking point in a very public way. During an interview with radio host Pete Dominick, Sanchez finally let loose. First he pegged Stewart as being an "elite Northeast establishment liberal" who had no idea what it was like to grow up in a lower-middle-class household, and then he let the big guns loose.

"I grew up not speaking English, dealing with real prejudice every day as a kid," he said. "I watched my dad work in a factory, wash dishes, drive a truck, get spit on. I've been told that I can't do certain things in life simply because I was a Hispanic.

"Deep down, when [Stewart] looks at a guy like me, he sees a guy automatically who belongs in the second tier, and not the top tier," said Sanchez. "I think Jon Stewart's a bigot. I think he looks at the world through his mom, who was a schoolteacher, and his dad, who was a physicist or something like that. Great, I'm so happy that he grew up in a suburban middle-class New Jersey home with everything you could ever imagine."

Perhaps Sanchez was unaware that Dominick was friends with both Colbert and Stewart and worked on both shows as the comedian who would warm up the audience before the taping began. It's also possible that if Sanchez had stopped with just criticizing Stewart, perhaps he'd still be working at CNN. Instead he continued to not only rail on Stewart but his own bosses at the network. "I'm telling you that everybody who runs CNN is a lot like Stewart, and a lot of people who run all the other networks are a lot like Stewart, and to imply that somehow they, the people in this country who are Jewish, are an oppressed minority? I can't see somebody not getting a job somewhere because they're Jewish."

The reaction was swift. CNN fired him the next day, but for his part, Stewart reached out to Sanchez, whom he said had misunderstood why Stewart had latched on to him. According to Sanchez, Stewart told him, "I made fun of you because you're the one I *liked.*"

In time, Sanchez's view of the comedian grew more nuanced. "I think Jon Stewart is misunderstood by a lot of people, and I say that as someone who misunderstood him myself," he said. "There isn't a 'real' Jon Stewart and another hiding behind comedy. It's . . . the same person. He's an equal-opportunity comedian [with] a simple, unified message and focus: he is opposed to extremes."

The reason why Stewart pursued Sanchez as a target may well have been this: the Sanchez exchange occurred just eighteen months into the Obama administration, and while Stewart had gone easy on the president in the first stretch of his administration, it was clear that he was becoming disillusioned with the president's evolving record. And yet, he didn't want to encourage Obama's naysayers on the right—and even worse, an increasingly vocal faction within the Democratic Party—and so in targeting Sanchez it was as if he had admitted he had stooped to shooting fish in a barrel: it was an easy cheap shot at a TV reporter who Stewart had viewed as selling out.

In essence, Jon Stewart had become the accursed establishment, the same thing he had accused CNN of becoming: the "straight down the middle" cable news network.

Or as one critic put it, "Another night, another *Daily Show* about Fox News," wrote Tom Junod in *Esquire*. "The problem is that Democrats, with their perpetual disarray, are not as funny as Republicans, with their reality-bending unity, and that Stewart is left to nurse what is probably the most potent comedy killer of all: disappointment."

"You can see the strain in his interviews," said a former *Daily Show* writer. "It used to be, 'Hey, we're a comedy show.' Now it's, 'What we do is so hard.' And it *is* hard. One of the reasons I finally left is that we were running out of targets. I was like, 'Do we really want to make fun of *Fox & Friends* again? Really?'"

Eighteen months into Obama's first term as president, though, the bloom was definitely off the rose as far as Stewart was concerned. "Obama ran as a visionary and leads as a legislator, which has been the most disappointing thing about him," he said. "People were open to major changes, and they didn't get it. I mean, he was pretty clear about some shit: 'We're not gonna sacrifice values for safety. I'm closing Guantanamo.' [But] he's more than willing to sacrifice someone to the voraciousness of the news cycle than to any sense of what his narrative is."

Stewart even went on *The O'Reilly Factor* on Fox News of all places to express his disappointment, though it wasn't the first time he'd appeared there; the two have frequently gone on each other's show through the years. "I thought we were in such a place we needed a more drastic reconstruction, perhaps, a destruction of the powers that be. I thought this may be a chance to do that. I have been saddened to see that someone who ran on the idea that you can't expect to get different results with the same people in the same system has kept in place so much of the same system and the same people. There was a sense that, 'Jesus will walk on water,' and now we're just looking at it like, 'Oh, look at that, he's just treading water.'"

Despite his disappointment and outward criticism, on October 27, 2010, Stewart welcomed President Obama to *The Daily Show* as the first sitting president to come onto the show. The appearance was supposed to be a midterm check-in as to Obama's progress since he'd been elected, and the two spent the full half-hour gently chiding and joking with each other,

President Barack Obama appears on *The Daily Show* on October 27, 2010. *(Courtesy REX USA/Rex)*

although the exchange was as far from a typical Stewart interview as you could get, with Obama speaking at length without interruption from Stewart and the host failing to mug for the cameras as he typically did during his opening segment. After the show aired, Stewart would complain that despite prodding from him, the president didn't unleash his humorous side.

Indeed, correspondent Wyatt Cenac said that Obama was a "terrible improviser and Stewart sort of likes to improvise these jokes."

In the end, perhaps the most poignant aspect to come out of the segment was that both concurred that changing America was harder than it initially looked when Obama first came to office:

"'Yes we can,' given certain conditions," said Stewart.

"'Yes we can,' but it's not gonna happen overnight," the president replied.

. . .

To temper the everyday sameness of producing a grueling schedule of a show four nights a week, Stewart continued to pull back a bit and turn to other projects, all radically different from one another.

First, in early 2010 he announced that he had purchased the film options to the life story of Maziar Bahari, an Iranian-Canadian journalist and filmmaker who was arrested by the Iranian government on suspicion of being a spy, a suspicion that had originated in a *Daily Show* segment from 2009 where correspondent Jason Jones—dressed as a spy—interviewed him. Once Bahari returned to Iran, he was held at the notorious Evin Prison—"every Iranian's nightmare," as another detained journalist called it—where he was tortured and interrogated for 118 days before his release. He returned to London and wrote a book about his time in prison and also incorporated his family history into the story. *Then They Came for Me* was published in 2011 and hit the *New York Times* best-seller list; Bahari also appeared on the June 6, 2011, episode of *The Daily Show*, in part to promote the book. Stewart started to write the screenplay and also planned to produce and direct the film.

"One of the things that appealed to me about the story is that it does have lighter moments," said Stewart. "One of the things that kept Maziar alive was his ability to keep his sense of humor—to remember about joy and laughter—and see the absurdity of his situation."

Next, *Earth (The Book): A Visitor's Guide to the Human Race*, was published in September 2010, the second book Stewart created with his *Daily Show* roster of writers. He welcomed the novelty of writing the book in contrast to writing for the show. "The show can feel very ephemeral," he said. "You work really, really hard every day to put it out there, and some days you're successful with it and some days you're not. That can be forgiving as a process, but there's not much time to savor anything either."

Just like its predecessor *America (The Book)*, *Earth* hit the top of the *New York Times* bestsellers list the first week it came out. The premise of the book was to serve as a guide to help aliens understand earthlings—who, by the way, have become extinct according to the book—again patterned after a standard high school textbook. *Publishers Weekly* gave the book a starred review, writing, "In place of skits there are elaborate, color illustrations accompanied by captions written with his trademark deadpan humor; for instance, a photo of a mother and baby elephant holds the caption, 'advances in contraception and industrialized food production allowed modern couples to have fewer offspring, while leaving the total weight of families constant.'"

New York Times critic Janet Maslin recommended the book, albeit with a few reservations. "The book, like the show, is best when it takes on subjects of real substance," she wrote. "The funniest material is about religion and science . . . the calendar of December religious holidays for all persuasions [and] the claim that the word Torah is 'German for kindling.'"

Yet other reviewers weren't as impressed. "The main problem might be the conception itself," noted critic Steve Weinberg in the *Christian Science Monitor.* "A posthumous pseudo-document for discovery in the future by vaguely imagined aliens probably seemed like a superb idea when conceived. But it is actually an idea that stretches credulity, even in a book that does not need to feel 'real.'"

Meanwhile, Stewart maintained his regular schedule of putting out *The Daily Show*. "Free time is death to the anxious, and thank goodness I don't have any of it right now," he said. He was also thinking of another project, and though he knew it was a long shot, Stewart began to openly ponder the idea of launching his own news network, one that would stray from *The Daily Show*'s formula of fake news and deliver real news through a filter that was not found anywhere on television.

"If somebody wanted to start a twenty-four-hour news network that would focus on corruption and governance as opposed to the politics of it, do you think that that would have a chance to be successful and change the way debate occurs in the States?" he asked.

In lieu of starting his own news network, Stewart opted to take a baby step in the interim by instead launching the Rally to Restore Sanity, which most people saw as a satirical response to a "Restoring Honor" event that Fox News commentator Glenn Beck held in August 2010. Beck's rally went head-to-head against another rally managed by Al Sharpton that same day to honor the Great March on Washington that Martin Luther King, Jr., spearheaded forty-seven years earlier.

"The rally is like everything that we do, it's merely a construct," Stewart said. "It's just a format in the same way that the book is a format or the show is a format. [They all] translate the type of expression that we do, and it's to be filled with the type of material that Stephen and I do, and the point of view."

Though Stewart's rally began as a joke on his show, public support quickly grew and Colbert joined in with his idea for a simultaneous March to Keep Fear Alive rally. The two promoted their respective events on their shows, and soon crowd estimates grew to almost seventy thousand people—thanks to a Facebook page set up for the event—which necessitated moving the rallies from the Washington Monument to the National Mall.

In promoting the rally, Stewart maintained that it was intended to send the message that the vast majority of Americans—from 70 to 80 percent—who are more moderate in their political beliefs, get drowned out by the vocal and extreme minority. He coined the rally's official slogan: "Take it down a notch for America."

"That was the point of the rally," he said, "to deflate that idea that that's a real conflict: red vs. blue, Democrat vs. Republican. I feel like there's a bigger difference between people with kids and people who don't have kids than between red states and blue states."

As news and plans for the rally started to unfold—along with requests for press passes from media from around the world—people who couldn't attend planned for their own rallies to occur simultaneously with the D.C. event. Even President Obama weighed in on the event, saying he was "amused" when he first heard about the rally. And both Colbert and Stewart took advantage of the interest to encourage attendees to donate to several nonprofit organizations, including DonorsChoose.org—a favorite charity of Colbert's where public school teachers post classroom projects that need funding and people can donate money online—and the Trust for the National Mall.

Celebrities from Sheryl Crow to Ozzy Osbourne showed up, and the artist formerly known as Cat Stevens, now called Yusuf Islam—who rarely performed in public since officially retiring from the music business following his conversion to Islam in 1977—sang his signature anthem "Peace Train" with Stewart. But the gist of the show consisted of Stewart and Colbert in ramped-up versions of both their characters, building their individual cases—Stewart for the middle ground and reason, Colbert for encouraging people to be fearful of everything under the sun, as dictated by both media pundits and politicians alike—before Stewart took the mike and addressed the crowd in an artful, heartfelt speech that caught many in the crowd off guard, since it showed a sincerity rarely glimpsed on *The Daily Show*, last seen during his opening monologue on the first show after returning to the air after September 11, 2001.

"The press can hold its magnifying glass up to our problems, bringing them into focus, illuminating issues heretofore unseen, or they can use that magnifying glass to light ants on fire and then perhaps host a week of shows on the sudden, unexpected flaming ant epidemic," he told the crowd. "If we amplify everything, we hear nothing. The press is our immune system. If it overreacts to everything, we actually get sicker . . . and perhaps eczema."

Not surprisingly, he then turned his attention to politicians and the government. "We hear every damn day about how fragile our country is, on the brink of catastrophe, torn by polarizing hate, and how it's a shame that we can't work together to get things done, but the truth is we do," he continued. "We work together to get things done every damn day. Most Americans don't live their lives solely as Democrats,

Republicans, liberals, or conservatives. Americans live their lives more as people that are just a little bit late for something they have to do, often something they do not want to do. But they do it, impossible things every day that are only made possible through the little, reasonable compromises we all make."

For the first time in his life, in that fifteen-minute speech, Jon Stewart finally revealed a little bit of the man behind the desk. "After twelve years, [I felt] I'd earned a moment to tell people who I was."

On the day of the rally, officials estimated the crowd at 215,000, which far outnumbered the estimated 87,000 attendees at Beck's rally.

While Stewart was overwhelmed by the response and support at the rally, he was also surprised when a realization bubbled up from out of nowhere while he addressed the crowd. "When you're standing at a rally and there are a hundred thousand people . . . [t]here's an incredible urge to go, 'I have the answer! Follow me!'" he admitted.

At the same time, he clearly understood that while many people thought Stewart was stepping out from behind his desk because he could clearly have a big effect and change some vital component of either politics or the media, that was never his intention in planning the rally. "I can understand the frustration of people who would be in that audience and think, 'you've been complaining for twelve years, this is your chance to stop whining and do something,'" he said.

Afterward, he had to run interference and reinterpret his aims for the media, because some people—at the rally and those who viewed it on TV—misinterpreted his intentions, perhaps thinking he was presenting a serious event to encourage people to get involved in politics. Some even ventured to guess that Stewart was using the rally as a way to test the waters for his own future political campaign, but all along he maintained that it was meant to be no more than a parody while spotlighting his view that most people agree with "the idea that the conflict [in America] is left versus right when it's actually corruption versus not-corruption." And though Stewart's political leanings are crystal clear to even an occasional *Daily Show* viewer, he wanted to convey the idea that neither left nor right is blameless since "both sides have their ways of shutting down debate."

So he made a rare appearance on *The Rachel Maddow Show* on MSNBC a couple of weeks later to clear things up, but if anything, he only ended up muddying the waters further. "Whenever you go out there, whatever you put out, you can only control your intention," he told Maddow. "You can't control its perception or how people receive it, [but] you *can* control your execution."

At times, things got a little testy between the two. "I feel like we're doing the same thing," said Maddow. "We both have a commitment to not lying, to telling the truth where we see it."

But Stewart clearly disagreed. "You're in the playing field; I'm in the stands yelling things."

In the end, the two came to an uneasy truce that was still filled with mutual admiration. And perhaps it was no surprise when Glenn Beck, the inspiration for the rally, weighed in, critiquing the Stewart/Colbert event as on the same level as "a high school play: not good," though he did acknowledge his admiration for Stewart. "Jon Stewart is very funny, and if I were in his position, I'd be doing a lot of the same things," said

Beck. "He takes things out of context—no worse than most of the other mainstream media—and is more interested in being funny than trying to actually understand the key messages in [my] show. I don't think he's looking for a Pulitzer, but his ratings are good. Good for him, keep doing what he's doing."

Beck maintained that Stewart was merely conveying the same message that he himself did in his August rally. But unlike Beck, Stewart was "co-opted [by the liberals]. I don't think he liked it . . . he was used," said Beck. "[When] the president himself promotes the rally, it becomes a mouthpiece for the [Democratic] Party, it became just another campaign stop. I don't think that's what Jon Stewart intended."

"Just because Jon Stewart makes fun of it doesn't mean he's right," said Jeff Zucker, president of CNN.

Still, Stewart's message was heard by some. MSNBC's Keith Olbermann revealed that he was taking Stewart's advice to heart and would discontinue his nightly "Worst Persons in the World" segment on his *Countdown* show. "Its satire and whimsy have gradually gotten lost in some anger," Olbermann explained. "So in the spirit of the thing, as of right now, I am unilaterally suspending that segment with an eye toward discontinuing it."

The criticism continued that Stewart was intentionally blurring the lines again. "There will be some commentators questioning whether Stewart and Colbert crossed the line from comedians to political commentators," said Pete Dominick, the commentator who had worked as the warm-up comedian for both Colbert and Stewart. "In all honesty, I'd say, yeah, I think they did make a political stance at the rally. The fact is comedy is an art form, and comedians are artists. You can't be passionate about something and not have some part of yourself and your beliefs shine through."

Yet again, Stewart denied it. "My job is to make jokes," he asserted. "I don't solve problems. If my job became solving problems, I would suddenly become a lot less good at what I do, unless the problem being had by the country was a lack of jokes."

There was one bit of criticism that he took to heart in the rally's aftermath. Author Salman Rushdie called Stewart to complain about having Yusuf Islam appear at the rally, since years earlier the singer had publicly supported the Islamic fatwa calling for the death of Rushdie, which had come about after publication of his best-selling novel *The Satanic Verses*, which many Islamic followers believe criticizes Islam and the Koran.

Yusuf Islam gave a speech at London's Kingston University in 1989 in which he said, "[Rushdie] must be killed. The Qur'an makes it clear: if someone defames the prophet, then he must die."

In an interview that same year, Yusuf Islam had said he'd be willing to carry out the execution of Rushdie if "ordered by a judge or authority to carry out such an act." When questioned about a demonstration where a group planned to burn Rushdie in effigy, Islam commented, "I would have hoped that it'd be the real thing."

After the rally, Stewart dismissed Rushdie's concern, to the author's great dismay, telling him, "I'm sure he doesn't believe that people should be put to death for apostasy. I'm sure the guy isn't really like that, let me talk to him."

He spoke with Yusuf, who initially denied that he agreed

with the fatwa, but soon shifted into his default mode of defense, asking Stewart, "Why do you have to insult the prophet?"

"We get into a whole conversation, and it becomes very clear to me that he is straddling two worlds in a very difficult way," said Stewart. "And it broke my heart a little bit. I wish I had known that, I wouldn't have done it, because that to me is a deal breaker. Death for free speech is a deal breaker."

At the time of their conversation, Yusuf had been booked to appear on both *The Daily Show* and *The Colbert Report*, but both ended up canceling his appearances.

Not all critics disliked the rally, though, and the two-hour live broadcast of the rally was nominated for four Daytime Emmy awards, including Outstanding Special Class Special and Outstanding Special Class Writing.

To further add to his workload, Stewart was helping his wife, Tracey, to launch and operate Moomah, a children's play space in Manhattan's Tribeca neighborhood which opened in 2009 that also offered art classes and workshops and a café with coffee and healthy dishes.

Despite being a celebrity wife, Tracey still found it difficult to navigate the city with a baby—or two—on her hip when her husband wasn't by her side. "Prior to having children, I loved going out to eat, being in my neighborhood, and visiting with my neighbors," she explained. "When I was pregnant, same thing. People open the doors and they're happy to see you, but the minute that baby is on the outside of you, they want nothing to do with you." She did the typical mommy-and-me classes and other activities, "dancing around with the

The Jon Stewart family goes trick-or-treating in Tribeca on Halloween 2009. *(Courtesy REX USA/Hector Vallenilla)*

baby and singing really terrible songs, but I wanted to shoot myself in the head," she admitted. If "the place was welcoming to kids, the music and food were terrible. I knew I wasn't the only one that was feeling like this." Thus, the idea for Moomah was born.

And she decided to add the art component to the café because she was unhappy with the kinds of children's art classes that were offered in her neighborhood. "I started to get frustrated with what was being offered to my kids," she said. "I would send my kids out to an art class and they would come home with a piece of construction paper with some glitter on it and I'd [think], 'This is what you did with my kids' time?'"

So with Jon's blessing, Tracey opened the kind of neighborhood place where she'd feel comfortable—along with her kids—and named it Moomah, which was what she had called the security blanket she had when she was a kid. "I wanted it to be like a security blanket for moms." And she decided to make creating art the focal point of the business partly because in addition to working as a veterinary technician, Tracey also had a background in art—she'd earned a degree in design and business from Drexel University and redesigned the lobby and offices of the Columbia University Clinic for Anxiety and Related Disorders—and partly due to her own anxiety issues. "Since I suffer from anxiety, the art projects help me find some peace of mind during the day."

From the beginning, Moomah was a hit. One reviewer said, "Moomah offers a killer parent-kid recipe: it's part café, part gymnasium, part art gallery, and part eco-exploratorium." And Jon helped out occasionally. "When we get in a bind business-wise, we always say, 'What would Jon Stewart do?'" said Tracey. "He advises us over the phone and has lots of ideas."

But the business soon ran into trouble and began losing tens of thousands of dollars each week, so Tracey decided to temporarily close the business in January of 2012 to regroup. "I couldn't get on top of my labor costs," she said. "I had a lot of teachers working who were staffing the art workshops all day."

Moomah didn't stay closed for long. "I was completely overwhelmed by the emotional response from my customers [when it closed]," said Tracey. "I didn't realize how much a part of the community it was." She radically scaled back from twenty-seven employees to just five, and scaled back the workshop hours along with the menu when she reopened the business in May of 2012.

However, just two months later, she decided to close the business permanently and convert the idea of the business—making a space where moms could make art and feel comfortable—to an online magazine at moomah.com.

As it turned out, her husband was in the process of gravitating toward the very same thing: finding a place where he could make art and feel comfortable.

Only he'd have to travel almost six thousand miles to do so.

CHAPTER 12

WHEN 2013 BEGAN, it was clear that Stewart was ready to head off in a new direction, at least temporarily. Though he had announced three years earlier that he had optioned the rights to Maziar Bahari's book and life story, he rarely mentioned it in public after the fact.

Until March of 2013, that is, when he announced that he'd be leaving for three months to direct the movie which now bore the title *Rosewater*. Though he had finished the script a couple of years earlier, he had had to wait on the financing; Stewart knew that once he got the go-ahead, he had to move fast.

In the first few years that Stewart was hosting *The Daily Show*, whenever he couldn't be on the set, one of the correspondents ended up sitting in the anchor's chair. Most of the time, that substitute host was Colbert—though Steve Carell also occasionally subbed for Stewart—and his success at the job inevitably led to *The Colbert Report*. After Colbert left, Stewart had changed course and decided to put the show on hiatus whenever he had to be away, usually just a week at a time, though the longest previous hiatus of just over two months occurred during the writers' strike of 2007–2008.

But an absence of twelve weeks from the airwaves was another matter entirely, and it was clear that Comedy Central executives—not to mention viewers—wouldn't stand for it. And so Stewart decided to appoint the *Show*'s "senior British correspondent" John Oliver as guest host for the entire time. Four weeks would consist of reruns, while Oliver would end up hosting for eight weeks in all.

Stewart was eager to pursue new opportunities away from *The Daily Show*, but it was also clear he needed a break. Some of his previous supporters now had issues with him, and could point out recent mistakes and missteps he'd made, in their eyes. For one, they started to criticize his knowledge of how government and policy works, and they were becoming impatient with what they viewed as his ignorance.

"Stewart seems weirdly unaware that there's more to fiscal policy than balancing the budget," said *New York Times* columnist Paul Krugman. "But in this case he also seems unaware that the president can't just decide unilaterally to spend 40 percent less; he's constitutionally obliged to spend what the law tells him to spend."

Jonathan Chait, a writer with *New York* magazine, piled on as well. "One of the habits [Stewart] has is to want to be bipartisan, but sometimes he misunderstands the way he needs to do that," said Chait. "Basically, you'll have Republicans in Congress do something objectionable, and the Democrats won't agree to it. Then he'll blame it on 'Congress.' It's not fair to criticize both parties in Congress when one side is doing something objectionable."

So when June arrived and he hosted his last show before the hiatus, it was a good time to get out of Dodge.

But that didn't mean stepping away from the desk would be easy for him.

When it came time to leave, Stewart was visibly nervous about his first attempt at directing a film. "I am a television person who is accustomed to having a thought at ten A.M. and having it out there at six thirty P.M. and then moving on, so this is a little scary," he admitted. "But one of the reasons we are in this business is to challenge ourselves.

"It's something I haven't done before, so I'm certainly coming from a place where I feel a lot more confident, or at least routinized," he said. "I'm moving into this area [that's new to me], so I thought the first day it might be nice to just sit in the chair and read *Filmmaking for Dummies* just to let them know that they are being led by an idiot boy. But I'm looking forward to it. It's a real good story."

Besides, as he had said many times before, it was in his makeup to be restless. "I like doing different things by nature," he admitted.

But in a way, the only thing that would change on the show would be the host. The production of *The Daily Show* had, by this time, become a well-oiled machine with not much left to chance. Perhaps that had been part of the problem the critics had noticed: it had become way too predictable.

"Everything will fundamentally stay the same, in terms of the way that the show runs," said Oliver. "Jon built it to operate in a certain process, so that process really has to stay. It's like a NASCAR driver giving keys to his car to a member of his pit crew. I fundamentally understand how the engine works—I just never have driven it that fast before."

Nevertheless, Comedy Central executives were understandably nervous. "[Taking time off] is something that he's been interested in for a while, so we worked out a way to accommodate it," said Kent Alterman, programming chief at Comedy Central. "We're interested in him being fulfilled and happy here, so nobody ever told him, 'You can't do this,' and we know he takes the show very seriously. There was a shared feeling between Jon and us that John Oliver made the most sense to fill in."

"I'm fortunate to have the type of people who have been producing it," said Stewart. "We've been there almost fifteen years, and Oliver is top-notch. He's a guy who has all the tools. He's so ready to do this, I don't think they'll miss a beat. If anything, he'll bring a nice British sophistication. It will be like *Upstairs, Downstairs* where everybody has been downstairs for a long time and now we're going to get to go upstairs."

In the seven years that Oliver had been a correspondent on the show, he had risen to the top of the heap, just as Colbert had done years earlier. And like Stewart, he was a news junkie. He kept his TV on at home all the time, though in order to keep a happy home life with his wife, Kate Norley, a veteran of the Iraq War, he learned to turn it off at night.

Oliver was excited but equally nervous about his hosting debut. "I'm looking forward to it in the way someone looks forward to a bungee jump," said Oliver. "I know it will be a fun and exciting experience, but I'm just not a hundred percent sure I should be doing it. But it's a real honor to be able to do this for him, however misplaced that trust."

He was also uncertain about how the set of the *Show* would

feel without Stewart. "He's a large part of our lives here, and the prospect of not having him around is a dislocating feeling," Oliver admitted.

At the same time, Oliver had spent enough time on the set that he was fully aware of how the show operated on a day-to-day basis. "Jon has always told us [that] you want to make sure that the spine of the argument is in shape," he said. "You can write jokes at any point of the day. Jokes are not that hard to write, or they shouldn't be when it is literally your job. It's harder to shift the point of view of a headline later in the day. That's the kind of thing you need to keep an eye on early. You'd think you'd come in early in the day and go, 'What jokes should we tell?' And that's not always the case."

"This show is such a sausage factory, that you are only concerned with the next day," Oliver added. "I find it hard in my general life to think further than the week ahead. So I've not really taken any big-picture thought about it, other than survival. But I've never had a regular job till I moved here. So I still can't imagine not working here. It really is just a process of trying to get each show on."

On June 10, Oliver assumed hosting duties, and once he settled into Stewart's seat, he let loose: "Welcome to *The Daily Show*," he began. "I am John Oliver and let's all just acknowledge for a moment that this is weird. This looks weird. It feels weird. It even sounds weird."

Over the next three months, both he and the critics were surprised at how well he did. From the first week that Oliver filled in as guest host, it was clear Stewart had made the right choice. Critics raved about *The Daily Show*, something they hadn't done for a while. And some made no secret of the fact that they actually preferred Oliver over Stewart as the mainstay.

Perhaps more importantly, at least in the eyes of Comedy Central executives, the ratings during Oliver's tenure equaled Stewart's: his first week, Oliver's shows attracted 1.5 million viewers, the same as Stewart's.

Stewart began his time away from *The Daily Show* by meeting his Egyptian counterpart Bassem Youssef, who is regularly referred to as the Egyptian Jon Stewart. Youssef invited Stewart onto his show *El Bernameg*, aka "The Program." When Stewart appeared on the show in June of 2013, Youssef's show was the most popular show in Egypt.

Dr. Youssef doubles as a heart surgeon and got his start as a humorous critic of the Egyptian government—and journalists—by making videos of his funny diatribes in the laundry room of his Cairo apartment building and posting them on YouTube after the 2011 revolution known as the Arab Spring. He called the show *The B+ Show*, aka "B(e) Positive," after his blood type, and aired the first show in March 2011 while riots were still going on in Tahrir Square. "My program is a direct result of what happened in the revolution," said Youssef. Within a few months, his YouTube shows were so popular, garnering five million hits each, that a major Egyptian TV network offered him a show of his own, which quickly became the most-viewed show in the country, and it spread throughout the region.

It's clear Youssef regarded Stewart as a hero. He framed one of his favorite Stewart quotes—"I'm not going to censor myself to comfort your ignorance"—and displays it prominently in his office. "I love Jon Stewart, and I will never shy from the fact that he is a role model," he said, adding that while there are similarities between the shows, his is necessarily less-polished than the American version. "We are at a different stage in building our country," he explained. "Stewart is in a much more stable environment, a much more established democracy. Here, it is much harder to come up with the program."

In hosting Stewart on his show, Youssef was also returning the favor. He had appeared on *The Daily Show* on a visit to the States in June 2012. "I love the guy," said Youssef. "He's part of the reason why I'm here."

In addition to his name-recognition in Egypt, there were signs that Stewart's popularity was spreading throughout the world. Even though *The Daily Show* is only broadcast in a handful of countries—including India, Australia, Portugal, and the United Kingdom—millions of people could view his shows online through ComedyCentral.com and YouTube. And if their governments banned it, there were always workarounds online.

Perhaps not surprisingly, China has a growing audience for *The Daily Show*, although Stewart's increasing popularity caused the Chinese government to start banning the bootlegged and illegally downloaded broadcasts that are uploaded with hastily added subtitles to Chinese social media sites like Sina Weibo and Youku; often the addition of a new show crashes the sites. In the spring of 2013, Stewart reported on the air pollution in Beijing and made the comment, "Things may be bad, but at least we can't chew our air." The segment went viral across the country along with an online campaign for Stewart to produce a week's worth of shows in China.

Known by his Chinese name *Jiong Situ*, Stewart has become so popular that many people yearn for their own version of *The Daily Show*, which would be pretty much impossible under the current Communist government. "How wonderful it would be if we could also complain about our country like this," commented one Weibo user.

From all accounts, despite the fact that *Rosewater* was the first movie he directed, Stewart was the consummate professional on the set.

According to star Shohreh Aghdashloo, who played a gypsy queen on NBC's *Grimm* series, Stewart worked hard to make the actors and crew feel comfortable. The first day of the shoot, he acknowledged his lack of experience and apologized in advance to the cast for any mistakes he'd make. Though he turned out to be a very hands-on director, he knew enough to trust the actors to make their own decisions when it came to figuring out their characters' motivations and actions.

"The good directors allow you to do that," said Aghdashloo, mentioning that she was so impressed with his work that she told him he was a born director. With a budget of under $10 million, the movie was shot primarily in and around Amman, Jordan, with longtime Hollywood producers Scott Rudin and Gigi Pritzker helming the production team. But after just a week on the set, Stewart asked his producers to increase the film's budget. Even though actor Gael García Bernal, who starred as Che Guevara in the 2004 movie *The Motorcycle Dia-*

ries, had already agreed to play Maziar Bahari in *Rosewater*, shortly before filming began he had asked for more money. The other principal actors in the film were relative unknowns and the film crew relied on numerous locals to pitch in where they were needed.

And so adjustments were made on the fly. A riot scene involving eight hundred extras presented an issue because there was no money in the budget for the expense. "There was a lot of debate and chaos around what we should do," said Alaadin Khasawneh, who worked as a member of the production team and also played a prison guard in the movie. He and the team came up with an ingenious solution: they put out the word on Jordanian social media sites that extras would be paid with a hug by Stewart. "It was a big risk and a gamble, but it worked out. And it just goes to show how much Jon is loved in Jordan."

Bahari, author of the book *Then They Came for Me*, also spent time on the set and was very pleased with how Stewart handled his story. "I think Jon did a very good job with the film," Bahari said. "I'm excited to see what the final result will look like."

And García Bernal concurred. "It was the most incredible filming adventure I've ever put myself into," he said.

The shoot was complicated by the fact that part of the filming schedule occurred during Ramadan. "It was an intense five weeks because people were fasting," said Khasawneh.

As filming progressed through the summer, Stewart settled into his role. His schedule on the film prevented him from watching Oliver's work as his substitute, but he joked that "[Directing] has been exciting and invigorating, but weird as hell," he said. "And I don't watch *The Daily Show* because it's too weird. It's like watching someone have sex with your wife's desk."

What was even stranger was that, as Aghdashloo described it, there was "a line of beautiful girls" always waiting just outside the set, eager for a chance to meet Stewart in the flesh.

The film wrapped in August 2013, Stewart returned to the States, and reclaimed his hosting seat on September 3, 2013. Postproduction began on *Rosewater*, and though a distributor had not yet been lined up, Stewart announced that the film would be released sometime in 2014.

When Stewart returned to *The Daily Show*, he was tanned, rested, refreshed, and more than ready to resume his hosting duties. Still, speculation had now begun about when—not if—he would leave permanently.

Was his first hiatus indeed the beginning of the end of Jon Stewart's long reign on *The Daily Show*? And if he left, what could he do that could possibly match his accomplishments on Comedy Central? Depending upon how *Rosewater* did with the critics and at the box office, he could forge ahead with a new career in the movies, succeeding the second time around, this time behind the camera.

On the flip side, many people have floated the idea that a natural next step for Stewart would be in the world of politics. But as before, he denied that he had any desire to run for political office on any level, answering the query, as usual, with a joke. "I would consider it, but unfortunately, there are some photos of me that would preclude me even from working at the post office, quite frankly."

But he's also given a more serious, practical answer: "I make a lot of money writing jokes," he said. "I get to go home, nobody bothers me. I don't have to get people to vote on things."

Despite years of making people laugh, making people famous, and changing how people view the news media and politicians, Stewart retains an *aw-shucks* attitude toward the amount of influence he's wielded through the years. "I deny that I am powerful," he said. "Power implies an agenda that's being acted on. Every generation has had its people who stand at the back and make fun of those in charge. I'm not saying I'm powerless and in a vacuum, but if I really wanted to change things, I'd run for office. I haven't considered that, and I wouldn't because [comedy] is what I do well. And the more I move away from comedy, the less competent I become."

He cautioned that there was a good chance that *The Daily Show* would cease to exist once he made his final exit. "When I leave, I leave," he said. "My entire biology functions on a *Daily Show* schedule, so when that ends, it will be an enormous change."

As one of the oldest employees on *The Daily Show*—as well as holding one of the longest tenures—there was another reality that Stewart had to face. "There will come a time when I will be holding the team back, and I will have to hang up the sarcasm since I'm not able to do it as nimbly as I need to."

Fast forward a decade—or two—and he doesn't believe he'll still be in the same spotlight. "I'm not going to disappear, but I don't want to work this hard."

Stewart openly admits that the show and its relentless pace

has aged him, in a similar way to how presidents look considerably older after only a year or two in office. "Look what's happened to me in the ten years I've been doing it: I'd [look like] the Crypt Keeper at a certain point."

He admits that when he finally leaves *The Daily Show*, there will be a void in his life that nothing will be able to fill. "Without the show I'm just an old guy yelling at the TV."

"You just have to keep trying to do good work, and hope that it leads to more good work," he said. "I want to look back on my career and be proud of the work, and be proud that I tried everything. I want to be able to look back and know that I was terrible at a variety of things."

He also gives ample credit to his youthful soccer obsession for helping him get where he is today. "Comedy and hosting a talk show is about the closest thing to sports that I have found," he said. "You don't know the outcome, and it really is up to you to do your best. If you lose, you lose, but you lose with dignity. You didn't want to be good for a small player or a guy with no left foot. You wanted to be good, to take your best shot at the top guys and see how you came out."

"Being funny is the same way," he continued. "You never think about the fans or the audience, because it's not about that, though if you don't have an audience, you're screwed. It's about the act of writing jokes. The thrill is in the creation of the comedy, or the doing of it, just like it is with soccer."

After all, deep down, he still considers himself just a guy from Jersey. "I love it there to this day. What's not to like? You have cheesesteaks, sand, sun. It's great. There are places to bodysurf, bars, places to get your ass kicked by a biker with tattoos. In all honesty, I love the Jersey shore.

"The one thing I did that was great was I moved from Trenton, New Jersey, to New York to try and become a comedian," he said.

"And the one great thing I've done is try."

ACKNOWLEDGMENTS

Eternal thanks be to Superagent, aka Scott Mendel.

To be followed by everyone at St. Martin's, including Peter Joseph as well as Tom Dunne, Sally Richardson, Melanie Fried, Margaret Brown, Aleks Mencel, Christy D'Agostini, Kathryn Hough, Laura Flavin, Joan Higgins, and the late Matthew Shear.

Also great thanks to Seth Bookey, who was an immense help when it came to digging into the life of Mr. Leibowitz.

Finally, to Alex Ishii for still being good for something . . .

NOTES

Introduction

1   "little hairy man of comedy": Dennis McLellan, "He Has Faith in His Jokes." *Los Angeles Times*, May 27, 1993.

1   "man screaming into the camera": Chris Smith, "The Man Who Should be Conan." *New York* magazine, January 10, 1994.

2   "the court jester of the family": Manuel Mendoza, "Late Night's New Kid Faces the Real World." *Chicago Tribune*, September 23, 1994.

2   "too smart for that little body": A. J. Jacobs, "Jon." *Esquire*, July 2001.

2   "I'm nervous about everything": *Fresh Air*, NPR, September 29, 2010.

2   "gives Jews their comic angst": Maureen Dowd, "America's Anchors." *Rolling Stone*, November 16, 2006.

2   "because we're not in charge": Tad Friend, "Is it Funny Yet? Jon Stewart and the Comedy of Crisis." *The New Yorker*, February 11, 2002.

3   "than I should be": Stephen Thompson, "Interview: Jon Stewart." *AV Club*, November 11, 1997.

3   "it's going to fail": Ed Bark, "*Show* Time for Stewart." *Dallas Morning News*, January 10, 1999.

3   "and I don't like working'": Frazier Moore, "Jon Stewart Plans to Keep Pace with Quick-Witted *Daily Show*." *Seattle Post-Intelligencer*, January 14, 1999.

3   "and turn it into something funny": Bill Moyers Interviews Jon Stewart, PBS, July 11, 2003.

4   "I hope I'm not prying": *Larry King Live*, CNN, December 8, 2004.

4   "two of them had to be—no?": *Larry King Live*, CNN, December 8, 2004.

4   "something that will make you laugh": Theresa Bradley, "Solidly Stewart." ABCNews.com, November 14, 2002.

5   *"Who wasn't?"*: "Oprah Talks to Jon Stewart." *The Oprah Magazine*, June 1, 2005.

5   "coming from that perspective": Jon Stewart, "Jon Stewart on the Art of Self-Deprecation." *GQ* magazine, June 1999.

6   "It is all-consuming": Jim Sullivan, "Jon Stewart: Growing Up on MTV." *Boston Globe*, May 6, 1994.

6   "'You know what? Screw this'": David Segal, "The Seriously Funny Jon Stewart." *Washington Post*, May 2, 2002.

6   "what I was doing": *Fresh Air*, NPR, September 29, 2010.

7   "we want to *stay*": *Larry King Live*, CNN, December 8, 2004.

7   "always open an ice-cream store": Manuel Mendoza, "Late Night's New Kid Faces the Real World." *Chicago Tribune*, September 23, 1994.

8   "is mind-boggling to me": Lee Breslouer, "Giving Everyone His *Daily* Dose." *University of Delaware Review*, September 1999.

8   "sort of a dream life": Robert Strauss, "Jon Stewart: You Know, That Guy on the Tube Television." *Los Angeles Times*, November 30, 1994.

Chapter 1

9   "and actually played outside": Geri Richter Campbell, "Dish." *Jane*, January/February 1999.

10 . "'I can't complain'": Curt Schleier, "Timing Is Everything." *The Jewish Week*, October 9, 1998.

10   "helped me have big friends": Jeremy Gillick, "Meet Jonathan Stuart Leibowitz [AKA Jon Stewart]." *Moment* magazine, November/December 2008.

10   "made sense to me": Curt Schleier, "Timing Is Everything." *The Jewish Week*, October 9, 1998.

11   "make me recite prayers": Jeremy Gillick, "Meet Jonathan Stuart Leibowitz [AKA Jon Stewart]." *Moment* magazine, November/December 2008.

12   "'a pussy can I be?'": Tad Friend, "Is it Funny Yet? Jon Stewart and the Comedy of Crisis." *The New Yorker*, February 11, 2002.

13   "memories of breaking into showbiz": Ed Condran, "Stand-up Comedy Lifts Jon Stewart out of His *Daily Show* Seat." *The Morning Call*, November 26, 1999.

14   "she had to fend for herself": *Fresh Air*, NPR, September 29, 2010.

15   "go to Long Beach Island": Ed Condran, "Stand-up Comedy Lifts Jon Stewart out of His *Daily Show* Seat." *The Morning Call*, November 26, 1999.

15   "I was a weirdo": David Rensin, "Jon Stewart: The *Playboy* Interview." *Playboy*, March 2000.

16   "smart-ass versus smart": Robert Strauss, "Jon Stewart: You Know, That Guy on the Tube." *Los Angeles Times*, November 30, 1994.

16   "as the bell was ringing": Jeremy Gillick, "Meet Jonathan Stuart Leibowitz [AKA Jon Stewart]." *Moment* magazine, November/December 2008.

16   "Jews had to live alphabetically": Ibid.

17   "running around like idiots": Marshall Owens, "Jon Stewart Recalls Life as a Local Boy." *The Daily Princetonian*, March 23, 2000.

17   "very dogged when I'm unsuccessful": Brian Kilmeade, *The Games Do Count*. New York: HarperCollins, 2008.

19   "the mall bathroom that day": Cindy Pearlman, "Must Be Moving On." *Chicago Sun-Times*, June 20, 1999.

19   "everybody making fun of me": David Wallis, "Man of Style." *InStyle*, February 1999.

20   "the late seventies dug that, man": *Fresh Air*, NPR, September 29, 2010.

20   "to get my friends into fights": Dennis McLellan, "He Has Faith in His Jokes." *Los Angeles Times*, May 27, 1993.

21   "going to make sports my life": David Wallis, "Man of Style." *InStyle*, February 1999.

21   "ability to make people laugh": *Biography Presents Jon Stewart*.

21   "tend not to go into comedy": Ibid.

21   "eleven o'clock at night": Jim Sullivan, "Jon Stewart: Growing Up on MTV." *Boston Globe*, May 6, 1994.

21   "'If I spit from here . . .'": Allison Adato, "Anchor Astray." *George* magazine, May 2000.

22   "defend my increased military spending": Ibid.

23   "that I want to be": Jon Stewart, "Bruce Springsteen's State of the Union." *Rolling Stone*, March 29, 2012.

Chapter 2

25   "not what I thought it meant": Commencement Address, College of William & Mary, May 20, 2004.

26   "who just went by 'Trip'": J. D. Heiman, "Jon Stewart, The Comeback Comic." *New York Now*, December 13, 1998.

27   "best of my college experience": Al Albert, *William and Mary Men's Soccer.* Charleston, SC: Arcadia Publishing, 2010.

28   "I developed my humor": Meghan Williams, "Comedian, Alumnus Returns to College for Q&A Session." *The Flat Hat*, November 1, 2002.

28   "a very funny guy": Ibid.

28   "he was so quick-witted": Jeremy Gillick, "Meet Jonathan Stuart Leibowitz [AKA Jon Stewart]." *Moment* magazine, November/December 2008.

28   "as you write five pages": Steve Kroft, "Jon Stewart's Rise to Stardom." *60 Minutes*, April 22, 2001.

29   "chances are you get a B": Ben Domenech, "Jon Stewart: The SIN Interview." *Student Information Network (William & Mary)*, April 26, 2002.

29   "to discuss a toga party": Meghan Williams, "Comedian, Alumnus Returns to College for Q&A Session." *The Flat Hat*, November 1, 2002.

29   "Don't touch the carpet": "Nightline Up Close: Jon Stewart." ABC-News.com, November 12, 2002.

29   "some very attractive women in college": Jeremy Gillick, "Meet Jonathan Stuart Leibowitz [AKA Jon Stewart]." *Moment* magazine, November/December 2008.

30   "didn't let it bother him": Ibid.

30   "the most of the talent he had": Chris Weidman, "WM's Most Famous Alum, Jon Stewart, Spun Soccer into Success." *WY Daily*, October 25, 2010.

31   "they no longer called us gringos": Jeremy Gillick, "Meet Jonathan Stuart Leibowitz [AKA Jon Stewart]." *Moment* magazine, November/December 2008.

31   "that in itself was probably annoying": Ben Domenech, "Jon Stewart: The SIN Interview." *Student Information Network (William & Mary)*, April 26, 2002.

32   "The entire place is an elective": Commencement Address, College of William and Mary, May 20, 2004.

33   "an amazing amount of [lousy] jobs": Sheila Anne Feeney, "Heeeeeeere's Jon: MTV's New Talker." *Los Angeles Times*, October 26, 1993.

33   "store proprietor, and window cleaner": Megan Smolenyak, "Hey, Jon Stewart, Your Roots Are Showing." *Huffington Post*, February 25, 2013.

33   "the Pine Barrens would be there": Robert Strauss, "Jon Stewart: You Know, That Guy on the Tube." *Los Angeles Times*, November 30, 1994.

33   "through the fan and get trapped": "Nightline Up Close: Jon Stewart." ABCNews.com, November 12, 2002.

33   "It was insane." Robert Strauss, "Jon Stewart: You Know, That Guy on the Tube Television." *Los Angeles Times*, November 30, 1994.

34   "tell me to clean them out": Michael Kaplan, "New York's Mr. Schmooze." *TV Guide*, February 29, 1994.

34   "who couldn't commit to a relationship": Chris Smith, "The Man Who Should Be Conan." *New York* magazine, January 10, 1994.

34   "to create something I felt part of": "Oprah Talks to Jon Stewart." *The Oprah Magazine*, June 1, 2005.

34   "fuck this. I need stand-up": David Rensin, "Jon Stewart: The *Playboy* Interview." *Playboy*, March 2000.

34   "all on the same day": "Oprah Talks to Jon Stewart." *The Oprah Magazine*, June 1, 2005.

35   "you're not getting up the stairs": David Rensin, "Jon Stewart: The *Playboy* Interview." *Playboy*, March 2000.

36   "for the next seventy years?": Tad Friend, "Is It Funny Yet? Jon Stewart and the Comedy of Crisis." *The New Yorker*, February 11, 2002.

36   "the guy organizing the team": Robert Strauss, "Jon Stewart: You Know, That Guy on the Tube." *Los Angeles Times*, November 30, 1994.

36   "won't save a seat for me": David Rensin, "Jon Stewart: The *Playboy* Interview." *Playboy*, March 2000.

36   "too young for a dental plan": Alyssa Lustigman, "Jon Stewart Jimmies His Way into the TV Talk Show Door." *INsider Magazine*, Winter 1994.

36   "it was like a bombshell": David Rensin, "Jon Stewart: The *Playboy* Interview." *Playboy*, March 2000.

36   "the person to discourage him": *Trenton Times*, 2006.

37   "on a six-week lease": Alyssa Lustigman, "Jon Stewart Jimmies His Way into the TV Talk Show Door." *INsider Magazine*, Winter 1994.

37   "through the Holland Tunnel": Interview with Bruce Springsteen, *The Daily Show*, March 19, 2009.

Chapter 3

39   "balls to go up on stage": Lee Breslouer, "Giving Everyone His *Daily* Dose." *University of Delaware Review*, September 1999.

40   "this is who my parents are'": Jon Stewart, "Bruce Springsteen's State of the Union." *Rolling Stone*, March 29, 2012.

40   "find themselves caught in Yidlock": Curt Schleier, "Timing Is Everything." *The Jewish Week*, October 9, 1998.

41   "a guy in the audience yelled, "You suck!": Martha Frankel, "Cosmo Q&A." *Cosmopolitan*, January 1999.

41   "never to go near a stage again": Paul Colby, *The Bitter End*. Cooper Square Press, 2002, pp. 143–4.

41   "better than anything else": David Rensin, "Jon Stewart: The *Playboy* Interview." *Playboy*, March 2000.

42   "I have no regrets about it": Gail Shister, "Jon Stewart Says His Late-Night Show Is a Bit More Casual Than Others." Knight Ridder Tribune News Service, October 11, 1994.

42   "some leftover resentment at my family": Tad Friend, "Is It Funny

Yet? Jon Stewart and the Comedy of Crisis." *The New Yorker*, February 11, 2002.

42   "did whatever popped into my head": Martha Frankel, Cosmo Q&A. *Cosmopolitan*, January 1999.

43   "write my first forty-five minutes": *Fresh Air*, NPR, September 29, 2010.

43   "success on Adam, even back then": Cindy Pearlman, "Must Be Moving On." *Chicago Sun-Times*, June 20, 1999.

44   "It's almost self-medication": David Rensin, "Jon Stewart: The *Playboy* Interview." *Playboy*, March 2000.

44   "working for falafel money": Tara McKelvey, "Jon Stewart's Dirty Laundry." *Mademoiselle*, August 1994.

44   "open mikes for a plate of falafel": Theresa Bradley, "Solidly Stewart." ABCNews.com, November 14, 2002.

44   "it didn't actually make sense": Ibid.

45   "what to proceed with": Ben Domenech, "Jon Stewart: The SIN Interview." *Student Information Network (William & Mary)*, April 26, 2002.

45   "In some ways, it's gladiatorial": Dennis McLellan, "He Has Faith in His Jokes." *Los Angeles Times*, May 27, 1993.

45   "And not in a happy way": Jim Sullivan, "Jon Stewart: Growing Up on MTV." *Boston Globe*, May 6, 1994.

46   "and what am I doing?": Chauncé Hayden, "Jon Stewart." *Steppin' Out*, December 23, 1993.

46   "for the first four years": Steve Kroft, "Jon Stewart's Rise to Stardom." *60 Minutes*, April 22, 2001.

46   "Chuckle Hutch and everybody's hammered": Chauncé Hayden, "Jon Stewart." *Steppin' Out*, December 23, 1993.

46   "he was heading for something bigger": *Biography Presents Jon Stewart*.

46   "I just kept working at it": Chris Smith, "America Is a Joke." *New York* magazine, September 20, 2010.

46   "just stay in the game": *Biography Presents Jon Stewart*.

47   "you have this weird thing about mopping": John Sellers, "Gimme Stewart." *TimeOut New York*, December 10, 1998.

47   "a guy talking about his grandmother": Chauncé Hayden, "Jon Stewart." *Steppin' Out*, December 23, 1993.

48   "staying in my room and drinking'": "America's Anchors." *Rolling Stone*, November 16, 2006.

48   "pleasant a time as he'd expected": David Rensin, "Jon Stewart: The *Playboy* Interview." *Playboy*, March 2000.

48   "pretty low common denominator": Noel Holston, "Comic Is Casting about for a New Gig." *Minnesota Star-Tribune*, June 16, 1995.

48   "my girlfriend who was living there": Larry Getlen, "Our Possible Future Mayor . . . Maybe." CityScoopsNY.com, May 19, 2009.

49   "it was an actual job": Don Steinberg, "Laughing in the Streets." *Wall Street Journal*, November 1, 2013.

49   "a superhero with a cape": Jordan Zakarin, "Louis C.K.'s Home Turf." *The Hollywood Reporter*, November 8, 2012.

50   "a reality-based show and a sketch show": Dennis McLellan, "He Has Faith in His Jokes." *Los Angeles Times*, May 27, 1993.

50   "but she was right": Tom Phalen, "Endearing Jon Stewart Has Hit the Mainstream after MTV." *Seattle Times*, March 23, 1995.

50   "people vomiting on animals": Sheila Anne Feeney, "Heeeeeeere's Jon: MTV's New Talker." *Los Angeles Times*, October 26, 1993.

51   "quiet here if I don't talk": Chris Smith, "The Man Who Should Be Conan." *New York* magazine, January 10, 1994.

51   "like an audience with the pope": David Rensin, "Jon Stewart: The *Playboy* Interview." *Playboy*, March 2000.

51   "and you become a bigger star": *Biography Presents Jon Stewart*.

51   "no such thing as 'made it'": Ibid.

51   "they picked more experienced people": Sheila Anne Feeney, "Heeeeeeere's Jon: MTV's New Talker." *Los Angeles Times*, October 26, 1993.

52   "That can really demoralize you": *Biography Presents Jon Stewart*.

Chapter 4

53   "we can take in that environment": Dennis McLellan, "He Has Faith in His Jokes." *Los Angeles Times*, May 27, 1993.

53   "he's also very sweet": Jill Gerston, "MTV Has a Hit with Words by Jon Stewart." *New York Times*, March 13, 1994.

54   "than what you could have planned": Michael Kaplan, "New York's
       Mr. Schmooze." *TV Guide*, February 29, 1994.

54   "Beavis, Butt-Head and me": Jim Sullivan, "Jon Stewart: Growing
       Up on MTV." *Boston Globe*, May 6, 1994.

54   "of course, that I'm miked": Cathy Hainer, "Jon Stewart, MTV's
       New Host with the Most." *USA Today*, December 21, 1993.

54   "just being happy to be here": Gail Shister, "Jon Stewart Says His
       Late-Night Show Is a Bit More Casual Than Others." Knight Rid-
       der Tribune News Service, October 11, 1994.

55   "cat litter that needs to be changed": John Hughes, "X-Man." *Sun-
       Sentinel*, March 15, 1994.

55   "without being too MTV." Dennis McLellan, "He Has Faith in His
       Jokes." *Los Angeles Times*, May 27, 1993.

55   "seven minutes at a time": Alyssa Lustigman, "Jon Stewart Jimmies His
       Way into the TV Talk Show Door." *INsider Magazine*, Winter 1994.

55   "off the air in six weeks": Jacob Hoye, *MTV Uncensored*. Pocket
       Books, August 2001, p. 136.

56   "He was off me": Ibid.

56   "to be hip and ironic": Susan Howard, "Nighttime Talk, MTV
       Style." *The Record*, 1994.

56   "a half-hour of my show": Manuel Mendoza, "Just Call Him the Un-
       Conan." *Dallas Morning News*, March 22, 1994.

56   "that the MTV audience recognized": Chris Smith, "The Man Who
       Should Be Conan." *New York* magazine, January 10, 1994.

57   " 'Are you gonna finish that?' ": Michael Rubiner, "Jon Stewart." *Roll-
       ing Stone*, January 26, 1995.

57   "we thought would work didn't": Steve Hall, "Jon Stewart Warms
       Up for Late-Night TV." *Indianapolis Star*, December 16, 1998.

57   "she was a little fresher": Jacob Hoye, *MTV Uncensored*. Pocket
       Books, August 2001, p. 136.

58   "it really blew me away": Jill Gerston, "MTV Has a Hit with Words
       by Jon Stewart." *New York Times*, March 13, 1994.

58   "never love or be loved": David Rensin, "Jon Stewart: The *Playboy*
       Interview." *Playboy*, March 2000.

58   "this really is a lot of fun": Jill Gerston, "MTV Has a Hit with Words
       by Jon Stewart." *New York Times*, March 13, 1994.

59   "into the walls, poor guy": Tom Phalen, "Endearing Jon Stewart Has Hit the Mainstream after MTV." *Seattle Times*, March 23, 1995.

59   "a big construction worker–looking guy": Lea Saslav, "Stewart Joins Late-Night Gabfest." *Orlando Sentinel*, September 13, 1994.

59   "have that much time": Michael Rubiner, "Jon Stewart." *Rolling Stone*, January 26, 1995.

59   "And it's sort of boring": Lea Saslav, "Stewart Joins Late-Night Gabfest." *Orlando Sentinel*, September 13, 1994.

59   "hide from your social life": Jill Gerston, "MTV Has a Hit with Words by Jon Stewart." *New York Times*, March 13, 1994.

59   "compassion and a sense of joy": Gail Shister, "Jon Stewart Says His Late-Night Show Is a Bit More Casual Than Others." Knight Ridder Tribune News Service, October 11, 1994.

60   "It's a really good environment": Phil Rosenthal, "Watch Out, Conan; Heeeeeeeere's Jon!" *San Diego Tribune*, January 31, 1994.

60   "while you're out there": Scott Williams, "Comedian Jon Stewart Enters the Talk Show Lists." Associated Press, October 22, 1993.

60   "sometimes puts us behind the eight ball": Chauncé Hayden, "Jon Stewart." *Steppin' Out*, December 23, 1993.

60   "the color of a manhole cover": Tom Junod, "Jon Stewart and the Burden of History." *Esquire*, October 2011.

60   "I shouldn't have shared?": Chris Smith, "The Man Who Should Be Conan." *New York* magazine, January 10, 1994.

60   "I can go on with grass stains": Tara McKelvey, "Jon Stewart's Dirty Laundry." *Mademoiselle*, August 1994.

61   "we were just bullshitting": Jennifer M. Wood, "The Jon Stewart Show Debuted 20 Years Ago Tonight." *Mental Floss*, October 25, 2013.

61   "and I never watch MTV": Phil Rosenthal, "Watch Out, Conan; Heeeeeeeere's Jon!" *San Diego Tribune*, January 31, 1994.

61   "being told to watch you": Ibid.

62   "don't be in show business": Gail Shister, "Jon Stewart Says His Late-Night Show Is a Bit More Casual Than Others." Knight Ridder Tribune News Service, October 11, 1994.

62   "getting married on the show": Lea Saslav, "Stewart Joins Late-Night Gabfest." *Orlando Sentinel*, September 13, 1994.

62   "It's right out there": Ibid.

63   "who thinks she's Underdog's girlfriend": Noel Holston, "Comic Is Casting about for a New Gig." *Minnesota Star-Tribune*, June 16, 1995.

63   "so we put it on": Michelle Farrar, "Aging Gracefully: A Few Gray Hairs? No Problem. Jon Stewart Has His Panic Under Control." *Axcess*, 1995.

63   "down a hallway with the fat-guy tape": Michael Rubiner, "Jon Stewart." *Rolling Stone*, January 26, 1995.

64   " 'OK, that's enough, we get it' ": Manuel Mendoza, "Late Night's New Kid Faces the Real World." *Chicago Tribune*, September 23, 1994.

64   "going to be killed that week": Tom Alesia, "A Funny Guy on the Fringe of Fame." *Wisconsin State Journal*, November 20, 1997.

64   "thinking about my laundry": Alyssa Lustigman, "Jon Stewart Jimmies His Way into the TV Talk Show Door." *INsider Magazine*, Winter 1994.

64   "the most difficult thing in the world": Tom Feran, "Jon Stewart Has Landed the Ultimate Gig." *Cleveland Plain Dealer*, September 2, 1995.

64   "what's going to happen to me": Michelle Farrar, "Aging Gracefully: A Few Gray Hairs? No Problem." *Axcess*, 1995.

65   "what you actually think": Michael Rubiner, "Jon Stewart." *Rolling Stone*, January 26, 1995.

65   "exhausted, emotionally raw": Michael Fleming, "Miramax Inks Stewart." *Daily Variety*, November 7, 1995.

65   "you're trying to avoid": J. D. Heiman, "Jon Stewart, The Comeback Comic." *New York Now*, December 13, 1998.

65   "and get back in it": Virginia Rohan, "Fresh *Daily*: Jon Stewart Takes Over Comedy Central's Mainstay." *Bergen Record*, January 11, 1999.

66   "What am I gonna do?' ": Rick Marin, "Nice Guy Finishes First." *Newsweek*, September 28, 1998.

66   "as I've gotten older": Michelle Farrar, "Aging Gracefully: A Few Gray Hairs? No Problem." *Axcess*, 1995.

66   "'Never confuse cancellation with failure'": Curt Schleier, "Timing Is Everything." *The Jewish Week*, October 9, 1998.

66   "with Cher, I'm happy": Steve Hall, "Jon Stewart Warms Up for Late-Night TV." *Indianapolis Star*, December 16, 1998.

Chapter 5

69   "keep the music down, they're fine": Michelle Farrar, "Aging Grace-fully: A Few Gray Hairs? No Problem. Jon Stewart Has His Panic Under Control." *Axcess*, 1995.

70   "sitting on a children's pillow": Allen Johnson, "Changing Land-scape." *Chicago Tribune*, August 18, 1998.

71   "'Who drank all my whiskey?'": John Sellers, "Gimme Stewart." *TimeOut New York*, December 10, 1998.

74   "an enjoyably dumb B movie": Steve Murray, "New on Video." Cox News Service, June 18, 1999.

74   "but it's fun to try": Ed Condran, "Stand-up Comedy Lifts Jon Stewart Out of His *Daily Show* Seat." *The Morning Call*, November 26, 1999.

74   "I held my own in this situation": Mari Burger, "You Can't Be Seri-ous." *Winston-Salem Journal*, January 28, 1999.

74   "and write your own stuff": Amy Longsdorf, "Jon Stewart, Over-achieving Underdog." *Bergen Record*, June 20, 1999.

75   "in movies playing other parts": *Biography Presents Jon Stewart*.

75   "that's a bit of a transition": Mari Burger, "You Can't Be Serious." *Winston-Salem Journal*, January 28, 1999.

75   "because you have to react to it": Michael Fleming, "Miramax Inks Stewart." *Daily Variety*, November 7, 1995.

75   "I'll be in the future": John Sellers, "Gimme Stewart." *TimeOut New York*, December 10, 1998.

75   "if people thought it was funny": J. D. Heiman, "Jon Stewart, the Comeback Comic." *New York Now*, December 13, 1998.

76   "than be who I am": Mark Bazer, "One to Watch: Jon Stewart Hangs In." *Boston Phoenix*, September 24, 1998.

76   "the character would need to do": Virginia Rohan, "Fresh *Daily*: Jon

Stewart Takes Over Comedy Central's Mainstay." *Bergen Record*, January 11, 1999.

77 "No one needs another halfhearted attempt": Tim Feran, *"Daily Chaos." Columbus Dispatch*, January 10, 1999.

77 "a bunch of different things": Allan Johnson, "Stewart Says He'll Settle Down—But Not Yet." *Chicago Tribune*, November 14, 1997.

78 "in interesting and unlikely places": J. D. Heiman, "Jon Stewart, the Comeback Comic." *New York Now*, December 13, 1998.

78 "He was a soft touch": Amy Longsdorf, "Jon Stewart, Overachieving Underdog." *Bergen Record*, June 20, 1999.

79 "at it as that different": Lee Breslouer, "Giving Everyone His *Daily* Dose." *University of Delaware Review*, September 1999.

80 "five of these jobs available": Linda Moss, "Stewart Takes Over *Daily Show* Reins." *Multichannel News*, August 17, 1998.

80 "Ted Koppel would want for Christmas": Monique Beeler, "Daily Showmanship." *Cal State East Bay Magazine*, Fall 2010.

81 "most talented free agent in the market": Linda Moss, "Stewart Takes Over *Daily Show* Reins." *Multichannel News*, August 17, 1998.

81 "very Ivy League and Midwest": Jim McConville, "Jon Stewart: Building His Own House at Comedy Central." *Electronic Media*, January 25, 1999.

81 "off the top of his head": Ibid.

82 "together with tape and string": Larry Bonko, "W&M Alumnus Steps into the Limelight." *The Virginian-Pilot*, January 11, 1999.

82 "give it time to evolve": Phil Rosenthal, *"Daily* Grind." *Chicago Sun-Times*, January 4, 1999.

82 "he viewed it as host-driven": C.J. "Winstead Walks Over Crudequips." *Minneapolis Star Tribune*, February 8, 1998.

83 "political humor, and surrealistic nonsense": Lewis Beale, "A *Daily* Dose of Irreverence." New York *Daily News*, October 7, 1996.

83 "and ten or twenty souls": Tad Friend, "Is it Funny Yet? Jon Stewart and the Comedy of Crisis." *The New Yorker*, February 11, 2002.

83 "savaged when the piece is edited": Jeff Macgregor, "Television; Past Jonathan Swift to Linda Tripp (Yeah, whatever.)" *New York Times*, August 23, 1998.

83   "come back with something funny": "The Daily Show's Stephen Colbert, Rod Corddry, Ed Helms, and Mo Rocca." *Onion AV Club*, January 22, 2003.

84   "good at reading the teleprompter": Benefit for Charleston Stage, December 23, 2007.

84   "bring passion, competence, and creativity to it": "Oprah Talks to Jon Stewart." *The Oprah Magazine*, June 1, 2005.

84   "He once seemed destined for more": Phil Rosenthal, "*Daily* Grind." *Chicago Sun-Times*, January 4, 1999.

84   "There are no mirrors": Virginia Rohan, "Fresh 'Daily': Jon Stewart Takes Over Comedy Central's Mainstay." *Bergen Record*, January 11, 1999.

84   "won't develop until I get there": Ibid.

85   "and start tailoring it to that": Ibid.

85   "take a shower afterward": Phil Rosenthal, "Daily Grind." *Chicago Sun-Times*, January 4, 1999.

86   "Not just celebrities, but newsmakers": Allan Johnson, "Changing Landscape Comedy Central Won't Come Up Short with New Host of *Daily Show*." *Chicago Tribune*, August 18, 1998.

86   "looking for where the ketchup is": Ed Bark, "'Show' Time for Stewart: Host Gets a *Daily* Forum for His Brand of Quick Wit." *Dallas Morning News*, January 10, 1999.

Chapter 6

87   "A welcome return": Frazier Moore, "Jon Stewart Plans to Keep Pace with Quick-Witted *Daily Show*." *Seattle Post-Intelligencer*, January 14, 1999.

87   "longer than four breathless minutes": Terry Kelleher, "*The Daily Show*." *People*, April 5, 1999.

87   "I forgive myself more easily." Matt Roush, "Roush Rave." *TV Guide*, February 6, 1999.

87   "in Kuala Lumpur, I'm Jon Stewart": *The Daily Show*, January 11, 1999.

88   "a rash like you wouldn't believe": Ibid.

89   "than I had imagined": IGN.com, August 11, 2003.

89   "now it's all confrontational": Douglas Durden, "Third Time's a Charm?" *Richmond Times-Dispatch*, January 9, 1999.

90   "The self-righteousness is embarrassing": Rick Marin, "Nice Guy Finishes First." *Newsweek*, September 28, 1998.

90   "and everyone goes over there": Jane Ganahl, "Comic Release." *San Francisco Chronicle*, April 23, 2002.

90   "your airbag could decapitate you?'": Seth Margolis, "Enough News to Keep 'Em Rolling." *New York Times*, January 10, 1999.

90   "we were a parody of the news": Peter Keepnews, "Late-Night Hosts in Search of Their Niches." *New York Times*, October 3, 1999.

91   "you don't really believe he's a news anchor": Ibid.

91   "to get in twenty monologue-type jokes": David Rensin, "Jon Stewart: The *Playboy* Interview." *Playboy*, March 2000.

91   "Our one rule is, no faking": Seth Margolis, "Enough News to Keep 'Em Rolling." *New York Times*, January 10, 1999.

91   "something we found interesting the day before": Gary Levin, "Fans Like Their Dose of *Daily* News." *USA Today*, October 6, 2003.

91   "the clearer our comedy becomes": Allison Adato, "Anchor Astray." *George* magazine, May 2000.

91   "it can be pretty ridiculous": Ibid.

92   "we'll be fine": "Writers Speak: A Potentially Regrettable Evening with the Writers of *The Daily Show*." Paley Center for Media, November 7, 2010.

92   "Oh, they're bringing him back!'": Terry Jackson, "Jon Stewart Puts His Slant on *Daily Show* News." *Charleston Gazette*, January 9, 1999.

92   "'Can you believe this!?'": Mark Bazer, "One to Watch: Jon Stewart Hangs In." *Boston Phoenix*, September 24, 1998.

92   "somebody hits on just the right bit": Seth Margolis, "Enough News to Keep 'Em Rolling." *New York Times*, January 10, 1999.

93   "change the jokes or improvise": Sharilyn Johnson, "Jon Stewart Almost Quit *Daily Show* over 'Asshole' Coworkers." *Third Beat Magazine*, December 10, 2012.

93   "these people are insane": Ibid.

94 "I don't have a problem with that": J. D. Heiman, "Jon Stewart, the Comeback Comic." *New York Now*, December 13, 1998.

94 "but that makes my job easier": Douglas Durden, "Third Time's a Charm?" *Richmond Times-Dispatch*, January 9, 1999.

94 "a machine that can cope with it": Seth Margolis, "Enough News to Keep 'Em Rolling." *New York Times*, January 10, 1999.

94 "point of view that's different": Phil Rosenthal, "*Daily* Grind." *Chicago Sun-Times*, January 4, 1999.

95 "would take all the fun out of it": Geri Richter Campbell, "Dish." *Jane*, January/February 1999.

96 "it's going to fail": Ed Bark, "*Show* Time for Stewart: Host Gets a *Daily* Forum for His Brand of Quick Wit." *Dallas Morning News*, January 10, 1999.

96 "and wish you could say": *Biography Presents Jon Stewart*.

96 "a relaxing effect on his personality": Ibid.

97 "it's just a heightened performance": Daniel Schack, "Jon Stewart Q&A." *The Daily Northwestern*, February 19, 2001.

97 "I am able to do here": Janice Turner, "How Jon Stewart Became the Most Powerful Man on TV." *London Times* (U.K.), October 2, 2010.

97 "and it really doesn't matter": Daniel Schack, "Jon Stewart Q&A." *The Daily Northwestern*, February 19, 2001.

97 "receiving a gift from the gods": Amy Longsdorf, "Jon Stewart, Overachieving Underdog." *Bergen Record*, June 20, 1999.

98 "that related to her": Maureen Dowd, "America's Anchors." *Rolling Stone*, November 16, 2006.

98 "about most people you meet": Alex Strachan "Jon Stewart's *Daily* Grind." *Vancouver Sun*, October 2, 1999.

99 "you feel much better": Marc Peyser, "Red, White & Funny." *Newsweek*, December 29, 2003.

100 "I was bartending or had a show": Maureen Dowd, "America's Anchors." *Rolling Stone*, November 16, 2006.

100 "third-grade science fair in the first place": Dennis McLellan, "He Has Faith in His Jokes." *Los Angeles Times*, May 27, 1993.

100 "to find values is through religion": Jeremy Gillick, "Meet Jonathan

Stuart Leibowitz [AKA Jon Stewart]." *Moment* magazine, November/December 2008.

100 "we're raising the children to be sad": *The Daily Show*, September 18, 2008.

101 "which is a rare combination nowadays": *Biography Presents Jon Stewart.*

101 "for what's on people's minds": Ibid.

101 "and really understand the truth": Marisa Guthrie, "Schieffer: Stewart, Colbert Are 'Editorial Page Cartoonists.'" *Broadcasting & Cable*, February 8, 2010.

102 "looked for larger arcs in the comedy": Phil Rosenthal, "A Comic Koppel No 'Indecision.'" *Chicago Sun-Times*, December 15, 2000.

102 "to me than most things": *Biography Presents Jon Stewart.*

Chapter 7

103 "that's happening at the desk": Mediabistro.com, May 6, 2003.

104 "rewrites a lot of his own stuff": University Wire, April 4, 2002.

104 "I don't really fit into anything": Chauncé Hayden, "Jon Stewart." *Steppin' Out*, December 23, 1993.

104 "we started to focus on media coverage": Monique Beeler, "Daily Showmanship." *Cal State East Bay Magazine*, Fall 2010.

104 "the only news organization who should be here": *In The Mix*, PBS, 2000 Republican National Convention.

105 "And should help themselves": David Daley, "Where Youth Gets Its News." *Hartford Courant*, December 7, 2000.

106 "a kind of recognized, viable pundit": Phil Rosenthal, "A Comic Koppel No 'Indecision.'" *Chicago Sun-Times*, December 15, 2000.

106 "We all felt that way": *San Francisco Chronicle* podcast, January 16, 2006.

106 "Jon Stewart officially became a public intellectual": Jeremy Gillick, "Meet Jonathan Stuart Leibowitz [AKA Jon Stewart]." *Moment* magazine, November/December 2008.

106 "journalists would want to come and talk": University Wire, April 4, 2002.

107 "the whole thing is ridiculous": *Larry King Live*, CNN, December 8, 2004.

107 "the overt game that's being reported": Stephen Colbert, "Ten Years of *The Daily Show*." *Variety* magazine, January 20, 2009.

108 "it's messing up our shtick": *New York Times*, November 22, 2000.

108 "it's Jay Leno's joke": David Daley, "Where Youth Gets Its News." *Hartford Courant*, December 7, 2000.

109 "I can't wait to see what happens next": Chris Smith, "America Is a Joke." *New York* magazine, September 20, 2010.

109 "CNN feels like an opportunity squandered": Eric Bates, "Jon Stewart: The *Rolling Stone* Interview." *Rolling Stone*, September 29, 2011.

109 "This is the most important show ever": *Newsweek*, July 31, 2000.

110 "he's a very politically aware news junkie": Howard Kurtz, "The Campaign of a Comedian; Jon Stewart's Fake Journalism Enjoys Real Political Impact." *Washington Post*, October 23, 2004.

110 "Where do you come up with these numbers?'": "Jon Stewart Discusses Politics and Comedy," *Fresh Air*, NPR, September 30, 2004.

110 "or social-security reforms": Conor O'Clery, "The *Daily* Capers." *Irish Times*, February 19, 2005.

111 "It's why we don't lead a lot of marches": Chris Smith, "America Is a Joke." *New York* magazine, September 20, 2010.

111 "and then they'd leave": David Daley, "Where Youth Gets Its News." *Hartford Courant*, December 7, 2000.

111 "It doesn't matter": Ibid.

112 "Or they're home cleaning the gutters or something": Ibid.

113 "a high-functioning hermit": Tad Friend, "Is It Funny Yet? Jon Stewart and the Comedy of Crisis." *The New Yorker*, February 11, 2002.

113 "Don't you find that people contact you way more?": Ibid.

114 "meaty and muscular and fun": Suzy Byrne, "Jon Stewart Opens Up on the Joys of Three-Legged Dogs." Yahoo Canada, June 7, 2013.

114 "but it's also truer": Gloria Goodale, "Politics as Punch Line." *Christian Science Monitor*, January 20, 2004.

115 "Of course, you're going to listen to Jon": Ibid.

115 "but you'd also be missing half of our joke": Mediabistro.com, May 6, 2003.

115 "a relatively savvy consumer of information": Nolan Gawron, "The Daily Ho with Mr. Jon Stewart." *Weekly Dig*, December 11–18, 1990.

115 "There's no insidious plan": Monique Beeler, "Daily Showmanship." *Cal State East Bay Magazine*, Fall 2010.

116 "our show is uniquely positioned to do that": Ibid.

116 "We're suffocating in information": Gary Levin, "Fans Like Their Dose of *Daily* News." *USA Today*, October 6, 2003.

116 "what's particularly absurd of this moment or of this time": University Wire, April 4, 2002.

116 "with something interesting to say about it": Conor O'Clery, "The *Daily* Capers." *Irish Times*, February 19, 2005.

117 "you have adopted [Stewart's] credibility": *Biography Presents Jon Stewart.*

117 "completely different from what I do": Amazon.com, September 2004.

117 "We are the last stop of the disgruntled": Conor O'Clery, "The *Daily* Capers." *Irish Times*, February 19, 2005.

118 "because he hates to be laughed at": Tad Friend, "Is It Funny Yet? Jon Stewart and the Comedy of Crisis." *The New Yorker*, February 11, 2002.

118 "because we think we have anthrax": John McKay, "Stewart: It's Hard to Be Funny Again." *The Province* (Vancouver), November 12, 2001.

118 "To me, that's edgy": Ben Domenech "Jon Stewart: The SIN Interview." *Student Information Network (William & Mary)*, April 26, 2002.

118 "It means you're being talked about!": Tad Friend, "Is It Funny Yet? Jon Stewart and the Comedy of Crisis." *The New Yorker*, February 11, 2002.

119 "all the camera guys are pooping": A. J. Jacobs, "Jon." *Esquire*, July 2001.

120 "if you do it the right way'": *Biography Presents Jon Stewart.*

120 "to find light in darkness somehow": *World News Tonight*, 2003.

121 "You can't beat that": *The Daily Show*, September 20, 2001.

Chapter 8

123 "than people would imagine": "Jon Stewart Discusses Politics and Comedy," *Fresh Air*, NPR, September 30, 2004.

123 "our paper of record": Marshall Sella, "The Stiff Guy vs. the Dumb Guy." *New York Times Magazine*, September 24, 2000.

124 "our morning cup of sadness": *Fresh Air*, NPR, September 29, 2010.

124 "frequently end up on the show": "Writers Speak: A Potentially Regrettable Evening with the Writers of *The Daily Show*." Paley Center for Media, November 7, 2010.

124 "It's pretty laid out for you": Ibid.

124 "It gets stronger": Ibid.

124 "knowing what you need to attack": Ibid.

125 "There's plenty of food to go around": *New York* magazine, October 16, 2006.

125 "Even after that, probably a month of salads": Ibid.

125 "I am incredibly horny": Ibid.

126 "I call fairly frequently": *NPR Talk of the Nation*, March 1, 2004.

126 "better than the ones you plan more": "Writers Speak: A Potentially Regrettable Evening with the Writers of *The Daily Show*." Paley Center for Media, November 7, 2010.

126 "and it is petrifying": Lauren Weedman, "A Woman Trapped in a Woman's Body." Sasquatch Books, 2007, p. 10.

127 "triple-A game every time": Rob Feld, "*Daily* Life." Directors Guild of America, DGA.com, Fall 2008.

127 "I will answer you facetiously": Janice Turner, "How Jon Stewart Became the Most Powerful Man on TV." *London Times* (U.K.), October 2, 2010.

128 "because we love the guy": *Daily Show* Forum, televisionwithoutpity.com September 16, 2011.

128 "It's a harsh work environment": Monique Beeler, "Daily Showmanship." *Cal State East Bay Magazine*, Fall 2010.

128 "managing, editing, and moving toward showtime": Maureen Dowd, "America's Anchors." *Rolling Stone*, October 31, 2006.

128 "We can just put it out there": Bill Moyers Interviews Jon Stewart, PBS, July 11, 2003.

129 "I just have to face in the right direction": *Fresh Air*, NPR, September 30, 2004.

129 "with his feet up on the desk": Monique Beeler, "Daily Showmanship." *Cal State East Bay Magazine*, Fall 2010.

129 "a thought behind every joke": Chris Smith, "America Is a Joke." *New York* magazine, September 20, 2010.

129 "lay them back to back . . . giggle": Eric Bates, "Jon Stewart: The *Rolling Stone* Interview." *Rolling Stone*, September 29, 2011.

130 "that I've been trained for": "Jon Stewart Discusses Politics and Comedy," *Fresh Air*, NPR, September 30, 2004.

130 "But we've never met before!": *The Daily Show*, November 30, 2001.

131 "about the movie or about you": *The Daily Show*, November 21, 2013.

131 "might not ask you anything": Ibid.

131 "for a four- to six-hour period": *Fresh Air*, NPR, September 29, 2010.

132 "make a better fucking movie": Sharilyn Johnson, "Jon Stewart Almost Quit *Daily Show* Over 'Asshole' Coworkers." *Third Beat Magazine*, December 10, 2012.

132 "as a straight commentator or orator": Eric Bates, "Jon Stewart: The *Rolling Stone* Interview." *Rolling Stone*, September 29, 2011.

132 "singles and doubles in a freshman dorm": Paul Rogers, "A Bald Liar." *Boston Globe*, May 1, 2005.

133 "overall, it was very loose": Obrien phone interview, February 3, 2010.

134 "they'd toss a football back and forth": Zimmerman phone interview, May 4, 2010.

134 "they were friendly and laid back": Ganis phone interview, May 5, 2010.

136 "they would be mistaken": Claudia Kawczynska, "The Dogs of *The Daily Show with Jon Stewart*." *The Bark*, June–August 2012.

136 "grass and squirrels [inside]": Ibid.

136 "Dogs are therapeutic": Ibid.

137 "shouldn't take life too seriously": Ibid.

137 "have won the dog lottery": Brian Williams, "Gone to the Dogs: Behind the Scenes at *The Daily Show with Jon Stewart.*" *Rock Center with Brian Williams*, NBC, September 28, 2012.

137 "who runs the show loves Ally": Ibid.

137 "at the end of the day": Claudia Kawczynska, "The Dogs of *The Daily Show with Jon Stewart.*" *The Bark*, June–August 2012.

137 "without these dogs": Ibid.

138 "there weren't dogs walking around": Ibid.

138 "they are dealt with the right way": Suzy Byrne, "Jon Stewart Opens Up on the Joys of Three-Legged Dogs." Yahoo Canada, June 7, 2013.

138 "to have them around": Ibid.

139 "through laughter and acceptance on stage": Wiltfong phone interview, May 5, 2010.

139 "that lends itself toward happiness": Ibid.

139 "It's like a dysfunctional family": Black phone interview, January 21, 2010.

139 "what's going on in the world": Wiltfong phone interview, May 5, 2010.

140 "these guys are doing stupid stuff": Ibid.

140 "that's me being that Stephen Colbert guy": *Charlie Rose*, December 8, 2006.

140 "He wants to *honestly* mock": Ibid.

140 "But I have nothing to back it up": Maureen Dowd, "America's Anchors." *Rolling Stone*, November 16, 2006.

140 "really just want to get a laugh": Ibid.

141 "just get our work done every day": *Charlie Rose*, December 8, 2006.

141 "other correspondents engaged Jon in conversation": Wiltfong phone interview, May 5, 2010.

141 "Stephen was one of the few": Ibid.

142 "That's part of the business": Ibid.

142 "a good thing to feel as a performer": Ibid.

142 "lucky to get a one-year contract": Irin Carmon, "The *Daily Show*'s Woman Problem." *Jezebel*, June 23, 2010.

142 " 'It's sooo hard to keep women here' ": Lauren Weedman, "A Woman Trapped in a Woman's Body." Sasquatch Books, 2007, p. 14.

143 "that person without some support": Irin Carmon, "The *Daily Show*'s Woman Problem." *Jezebel*, June 23, 2010.

143 " 'Like how you talk to everyone but him' ": Lauren Weedman, "A Woman Trapped in a Woman's Body." Sasquatch Books, 2007, p. 20.

143 "And I knew I'd be fired": Ibid., p. 10.

144 "and all the Comedy Central executives": Ibid., p. 27.

144 "So it kind of goes both ways": Irin Carmon, "The Only Women in the Late Night Writers' Rooms." *Jezebel*, May 14, 2010.

144 "questions like I did yesterday": Ibid.

144 "They're miserable for everyone": Lynn Harris, "Late Night's Real Problem." *Salon*, January 10, 2010.

145 "a show that's all about men": Ibid.

145 "is always a dude": Bill Carter, "Among Late-Night Writers, Few Women in the Room. *New York Times*, November 11, 2009.

145 "three or four were from women": Ibid.

146 "it's based in frustration over reality": Maureen Dowd, "America's Anchors." *Rolling Stone*, November 16, 2006.

146 "we don't have to defend anything": Ibid.

146 "we very much infuse it with who we are": *Paley Center Daily Show* chat, April 19, 2001.

146 "the actual ethics of real journalism": John Crook, "Comics Mining Laughs from Presidential Race." *Rocky Mountain News*, July 21, 1999.

147 "that is driving the entire enterprise": *Biography Presents Jon Stewart.*

147 "he's mad at them for going union": Ed Brayton, Culture Wars Radio, May 15, 2012.

147 "But he doesn't have a mustache": *The Daily Show*, January 25, 2005.

147 "I try not to let him out": Tom Junod, "Jon Stewart and the Burden of History." *Esquire*, October 2011.

148 "what I'd do if he wasn't' ": Ibid.

148 "runs *The Daily Show* with joyless rage": Irin Carmon, The *Daily Show*'s Woman Problem." *Jezebel*, June 23, 2010.

148 "I didn't fit the core principle there": Wiltfong phone interview, May 5, 2010.

149 "I was getting this angry phone call": *Piers Morgan Live*, October 6, 2011.

149 "haranguing you for mocking him": Ibid.

149 "is creatively and physically exhausting": Louis B. Hobson, "Jon Stewart's Cookin' Now." *Calgary Sun*, June 26, 1999.

149 "until something's desperately wrong": "Jon Stewart Discusses Politics and Comedy," *Fresh Air,* NPR, September 30, 2004.

149 "but we are": Daniel Schack, "Jon Stewart Q&A." *The Daily Northwestern*, February 19, 2001.

150 "what our day is like every day": Chris Smith, "America Is a Joke." *New York* magazine, September 20, 2010.

Chapter 9

152 "this film creaks like a broken-down tractor": Kevin Smith, "Death by *Smoochy.*" *The Beacon News*, April 5, 2002.

153 "whatever's on my mind at the time": Dan Sweeney, "Heeeeere's Jonny!" *New Times*, February 27, 2003.

154 "to connect with the farmers": *Talk of the Nation*, NPR, March 1, 2004.

154 "and don't want to talk to anybody": Ibid.

154 "We never forget that we're not": Ibid.

155 "It's a Nerf interview": *Biography Presents Jon Stewart.*

155 "the focus of 22 percent of the segments": "Journalism, Satire or Just Laughs? *The Daily Show with Jon Stewart*, Examined." Pew Research Center's Journalism Project Staff, May 8, 2008.

156 "Bush is a gold mine": *Biography Presents Jon Stewart.*

156 "to be able to honestly mock": *Charlie Rose*, December 8, 2006.

156 "you can pretty much hammer away at anybody": Marshall Sella, "The Stiff Guy vs. the Dumb Guy." *New York Times Magazine*, September 24, 2000.

156 "some new material and some new challenges": "Writers Speak: A

Potentially Regrettable Evening with the Writers of *The Daily Show*."
Paley Center for Media, November 7, 2010.

157 "it so clearly goes against his constitution": *Larry King Live*, CNN,
December 8, 2004.

157 "and show him that I'm an idiot": Ibid.

157 "I don't think that's anything to honor or enjoy": Maureen Dowd,
"America's Anchors." *Rolling Stone*, November 16, 2006.

158 "The paradigm has switched": *Larry King Live*, CNN, June 25, 2004.

158 "politics are handled within the media": Howard Kurtz, "The Campaign of a Comedian; Jon Stewart's Fake Journalism Enjoys Real Political Impact." *Washington Post*, October 23, 2004.

158 "is that it's cathartic": Ibid.

159 "very strong driver of our revenue": Alice Z. Cuneo, "Marketers, Politicians Clamor for *Daily* Fix." *Advertising Age*, September 27, 2004.

159 "that really has found a niche": Ibid.

160 "this is the way *real* journalism should be": Wiltfong phone interview, May 5, 2010.

160 "a personal kick in the [balls]": Frazier Moore, "Jon Stewart, Daily
Show, Cover America in New Book." *Charleston Daily Mail*, October
14, 2004.

162 "hurting America." *Crossfire*, October 14, 2004.

162 "to be your monkey": Ibid.

162 "was kind of embarrassed for him": *Biography Presents Jon Stewart*.

163 "This was real.": Ibid.

163 "news stories on the Associated Press": *Scarborough Country*, September 27, 2006.

163 "sometimes they break news": Ibid.

163 "sort of pin in the balloon": Frazier Moore, "Jon Stewart Plans to
Keep Pace with Quick-Witted *Daily Show*." *Seattle Post-Intelligencer*,
January 14, 1999.

164 "with the same respect": David Bauder, "CNN Lets *Crossfire* Host
Carlson Go." Associated Press, January 5, 2005.

165 "the kid in the back throwing spitballs": Howard Kurtz, "The Campaign of a Comedian; Jon Stewart's Fake Journalism Enjoys Real Political Impact." *Washington Post*, October 23, 2004.

165 "they do the satirical Jon": Bill Carter & Brian Stelter, "In *Daily Show* Role on 9/11 Bill, Echoes of Murrow." *New York Times*, December 26, 2010.

165 "He's a necessary branch of government": Chris Smith, "America Is a Joke." *New York* magazine, September 20, 2010.

165 "'I'm just a satirist'": Howard Kurtz, "The Campaign of a Comedian; Jon Stewart's Fake Journalism Enjoys Real Political Impact." *Washington Post*, October 23, 2004.

166 "that's really all right": *Larry King Live*, CNN, February 27, 2006.

166 "CBS should have been doing": Jeremy Gillick, "Meet Jonathan Stuart Leibowitz [AKA Jon Stewart]." *Moment* magazine, November/December 2008.

166 "the new millennium without *The Daily Show*": Bill Moyers Interviews Jon Stewart, PBS, July 11, 2003.

167 "do this again somewhere": *The Daily Show*, October 29, 2002.

167 "any credibility to lose": Conor O'Clery, "The *Daily* Capers." *Irish Times*, February 19, 2005.

167 "I'd like that. I'm tired": *The Daily Show*, November 1, 2004.

168 "why is this guy still on the show?": Wiltfong phone interview, May 5, 2010.

168 "I didn't want to *not* like it": Adam Sternbergh, "Stephen Colbert Has America by the Ballots." *New York* magazine, October 16, 2006.

169 "someone like Stephen could do": Seth Mnookin, "The Man in the Irony Mask." *Vanity Fair*, October 2007.

170 "But I can't be an asshole": Adam Sternbergh, "Stephen Colbert Has America by the Ballots." *New York* magazine, October 16, 2006.

170 "You're an idiot. There's a difference": Ibid.

170 "because we hid his keys": Howard Kurtz, "TV's Newest Anchor: A Smirk in Progress." *Washington Post*, October 10, 2005.

170 "It's really a virtuoso performance": Seth Mnookin, "The Man in the Irony Mask." *Vanity Fair*, October 2007.

170 "doing his show in a second language": Ibid.

171 "very contented and warm feeling": Marc Peyser, "Red, White & Funny." *Newsweek*, December 29, 2003.

Chapter 10

174 "coming across as mean-spirited or nasty": Gary Levin, "Jon Stewart Looks Oscar in the Eye." *USA Today*, February 19, 2006.

174 "I was losing my mind": Ibid.

174 "I don't have any of it right now": Ibid.

174 "and Dick Cheney shot her": 78th Academy Awards, March 5, 2006.

175 "pale shadow of great hosts gone by": Tom Shales, "Memo to Jon Stewart: Keep Your Daily Job." *Washington Post*, March 6, 2006.

175 "as he usually is": Alessandra Stanley, "The Dresses, Low Cut, but the Tones Were Lofty." *New York Times*, March 6, 2006.

175 "the Oscars is a really hard gig": *Biography Presents Jon Stewart*.

175 "after a game of musical chairs": Gary Susman, "Oscar Hosts: From Worst to Best, Rating 60 Years of Academy Awards Emcees." Moviefone.com, February 16, 2012.

176 "it was such a bad job": *Biography Presents Jon Stewart*.

176 "laugh impulse has been deadened": Adam Sternbergh, "Because What's the Point of Being Funny in Wisconsin?" *New York* magazine, October 24, 2007.

176 "The sky's the limit": Nathan Rabin, AV Club, October 12, 2006.

177 "it was at least surprising": Jaime J. Weinman, "What's Happened to *The Daily Show*?" *Macleans*, January 22, 2007.

178 "and saying that it cures impetigo?": *The Daily Show*, March 12, 2009.

179 "I wish he'd get back to work": Letters and Comments, usanews.com, March 18, 2009.

179 "What am I going to do with that?": *The Late Show with David Letterman*, October 6, 2005.

180 "He's really all about his family": Lisa Fickenscher, "Cooking Up a Café Comeback." *Crain's New York Business*, June 3, 2012.

180 "to thermonuclear levels": Suzy Byrne, "Jon Stewart Opens Up on the Joys of Three-Legged Dogs." Yahoo Canada, June 7, 2013.

181 "and me on the inside": Kat Harrison, "The Mama of Moomah." *New York Family*, December 30, 2011.

183   "to be the case": *The Daily Show*, May 1, 2009.

184   "not in a mean or nasty way": Marc Peyser, "Red, White & Funny." *Newsweek*, December 29, 2003.

184   "It's just cruel": Stephen Galloway, "Steve Carell Says Comedy Has Become 'Uber-Cynical,' 'Borderline Mean.'" *Hollywood Reporter*, August 2012.

185   "another congressman doing a dumb thing": Larry Getlen, "Our Possible Future Mayor . . . Maybe." CityScoopsNY.com, May 19, 2009.

185   "virtue and beacons of decency": *Larry King Live*, CNN, June 25, 2004.

185   "you didn't just ask me that.": Ibid.

186   "Where's Osama bin Laden?" *The Daily Show*, September 27, 2006.

186   "we'll follow you.": Ibid.

186   "they'd both lose miserably": Ibid.

187   "because they air four nights a week": *Multichannel News*, October 29, 2007.

187   "in terms of writing and performing material on the show": Ibid.

187   "What's your answer?": Associated Press, December 25, 2007.

188   "we are unable to express something as nuanced as ambivalence": Associated Press, December 21, 2007.

188   "or at least balance him a bit": Thomas Tennant, "*Daily Show, Colbert Report* Back Live." About.com Talk Shows, January 9, 2008.

189   "it is cathartic and energizing": Janice Turner, "How Jon Stewart Became the Most Powerful Man on TV." *London Times* (U.K.), October 2, 2010.

190   "hundreds of millions around the world": Gary Susman, "Oscar Hosts: From Worst to Best, Rating 60 Years of Academy Awards Emcees." Moviefone.com, February 16, 2012.

190   "the tone of the material": Ibid.

191   "for the first time ever, delivering a piece of real news": *Nofact Zone*, December 2, 2008.

191   "We're a fake news show": Ibid.

191   "I'm still afraid someone's going to take it away": Associated Press, November 5, 2008.

Chapter 11

194 "maybe I wouldn't have worked as hard": Eric Bates, "Jon Stewart: The *Rolling Stone* Interview." *Rolling Stone*, September 29, 2011.

195 "because I was a Hispanic": *Stand Up with Pete Dominick*, September 30, 2010.

195 "because they're Jewish": Ibid.

195 "because you're the one I *liked*": Tom Junod, "Jon Stewart and the Burden of History." *Esquire*, October 2011.

196 "he is opposed to extremes": Ibid.

196 "the most potent comedy killer of all: disappointment": Ibid.

197 "make fun of *Fox & Friends* again? Really?": Tom Junod, "Jon Stewart and the Burden of History." *Esquire*, October 2011.

197 "of what his narrative is": Chris Smith, "America Is a Joke." *New York* magazine, September 20, 2010.

197 "he's just treading water": *The O'Reilly Factor*, September 22, 2010.

198 "Stewart sort of likes to improvise these jokes": "Writers Speak: A Potentially Regrettable Evening with the Writers of *The Daily Show*": Paley Center for Media, November 7, 2010.

198 "it's not gonna happen overnight": *The Daily Show*, October 27, 2010.

199 "every Iranian's nightmare": D. Parvaz, "16 Days in Evin Prison." *Frontline*, PBS, January 25, 2012.

199 "the absurdity of his situation": Brooks Barnes, "Jon Stewart to Direct Serious Film, Will Take Hiatus from *Daily Show*." *New York Times*, March 5, 2013.

200 "not much time to savor anything either": *The Oprah Winfrey Show*, September 21, 2010.

200 "the total weight of families constant": *Publishers Weekly*, September 27, 2010.

200 "'German for kindling'": Janet Maslin, "In this World, Let the Farce Be with You." *New York Times*, October 4, 2010.

201 "does not need to feel 'real'": Steve Weinberg, "*Earth (The Book)*." *Christian Science Monitor*, September 24, 2010.

201 "I don't have any of it right now": Gary Levin, "Jon Stewart Looks Oscar in the Eye." *USA Today*, February 19, 2006.

202 "red states and blue states": *The Rachel Maddow Show*, MSNBC, November 15, 2010.

204 "to tell people who I was": *The Rachel Maddow Show*, MSNBC, November 10, 2010.

204 " 'I have the answer! Follow me!' ": Eric Bates, "Jon Stewart: The *Rolling Stone* Interview." *Rolling Stone*, September 29, 2011.

205 "ways of shutting down debate": *The Rachel Maddow Show*, MSNBC, November 10, 2010.

205 "a high school play: not good": *The Glenn Beck Program*, November 1, 2010.

206 "keep doing what he's doing": Chris Smith, "America Is a Joke." *New York* magazine, September 20, 2010.

206 "that's what Jon Stewart intended": *The Glenn Beck Program*, November 1, 2010.

206 "doesn't mean he's right": Terri Thornton, "CNN's Jeff Zucker Talks Social Media, Considers Native Ads." *Mediashift*, PBS, April 17, 2013.

207 "and your beliefs shine through": Pete Dominick, "Commentary: Path to Sanity Paved with Humor, Dominick Finds." CNN.com, October 30, 2010.

207 "was a lack of jokes": *The Oprah Winfrey Show*, September 22, 2010.

207 "then he must die": Speech, Kingston University, February 21, 1989.

207 "it'd be the real thing": Geoffrey Robertson, *Hypotheticals: A Satanic Scenario*. BBC, May 30, 1989.

207 "let me talk to him": Sharilyn Johnson, "Jon Stewart Almost Quit *Daily Show* Over 'Asshole' Coworkers." *Third Beat Magazine*, December 10, 2012.

208 "is a deal breaker": Ibid.

209 "that was feeling like this": Kat Harrison, "The Mama of Moomah." *New York Family*, December 30, 2011.

209 "with my kids' time?": Lisa Rogal, "Magical Moomah." *New York Family*, 2011.

210 "some peace of mind during the day": Lisa Fickenscher, "Cooking Up a Café Comeback." *Crain's New York Business*, June 3, 2012.

210 "and has lots of ideas": Ibid.

210 "staffing the art workshops all day": Ibid.

Chapter 12

214 "what the law tells him to spend": Paul Krugman, "Lazy Jon Stewart." *New York Times* blog, January 12, 2013.

214 "is doing something objectionable": Daniel D'Addario, "Is Jon Stewart Turning Off His Fan Base?" *Salon*, January 19, 2013.

215 "is to challenge ourselves": Brooks Barnes, "Jon Stewart to Direct Serious Film, Will Take Hiatus from *Daily Show*." *New York Times*, March 5, 2013.

215 "It's a real good story": Suzy Byrne, " 'Nervous' Jon Stewart on Making His Directorial Debut." Yahoo TV, June 5, 2013.

215 "different things by nature": Gary Levin, "Fans Like Their Dose of *Daily* News." *USA Today*, October 6, 2003.

215 "driven it that fast before": Dave Itzkoff, "Step Aside, Jon Stewart: John Oliver Prepares to Host *The Daily Show*." *New York Times*, June 3, 2013.

216 "the most sense to fill in": Lacey Rose, "Comedy Central's Kent Alterman on *Leno*, Rape Jokes, and a Jon Stewart–Free *Daily Show*." *Hollywood Reporter*, May 1, 2013.

216 "get to go upstairs": Suzy Byrne, " 'Nervous' Jon Stewart on Making His Directorial Debut." Yahoo TV, June 5, 2013.

216 "however misplaced that trust": Gary Levin, "John Keeps Jon's Seat Warm at *Daily Show*." *USA Today*, June 10, 2013.

217 "is a dislocating feeling": Ibid.

217 "that's not always the case": Dave Itzkoff, "Step Aside, Jon Stewart: John Oliver Prepares to Host *The Daily Show*." *New York Times*, June 3, 2013.

217 "get each show on": Ibid.

217 "It even sounds weird": *The Daily Show*, June 10, 2013.

218 "what happened in the revolution": Patrick Kingsley, "Meet the Jon Stewart of Egypt." *The Guardian*, March 6, 2013.

219 "come up with the program": Ibid.

219 "the reason why I'm here": Mike Giglio, "Egypt's *Daily Show*." *Newsweek*, March 8, 2013.

220 "our country like this": Leo Lewis, "*Daily Show* Satirist Is Helping the Chinese to Lampoon Their Leaders." *The Times* (London), May 25, 2013.

220 "allow you to do that": Kimberly Nordyke, "Noor Fest Honoree Shohreh Aghdashloo Talks Jon Stewart's Directing Style." *Hollywood Reporter*, October 24, 2013.

221 "Jon is loved in Jordan": Marie-Louise Olson, "Jon Stewart: A Man of the People in Jordan." *The National*, September 10, 2013.

221 "the final result will look like": Matthew Hays, "Reporter's Ordeal Includes Captivity, Torture, *Daily Show*." *The Globe and Mail*, October 2, 2013.

221 "I've ever put myself into": Tom Peacock, "Gael García Bernal's 'Incredible Filming Adventure.'" Concordia University, November 26, 2013.

221 "because people were fasting": Marie-Louise Olson, "Jon Stewart: A Man of the People in Jordan." *The National*, September 10, 2013.

222 "have sex with your wife's desk": Hilary Lewis, "Jon Stewart Misses *The Daily Show*." *The Hollywood Reporter*, June 28, 2013.

222 "a line of beautiful girls": Kimberly Nordyke, "Noor Fest Honoree Shohreh Aghdashloo Talks Jon Stewart's Directing Style." *Hollywood Reporter*, October 24, 2013.

222 "at the post office, quite frankly": *Larry King Live*, CNN, June 25, 2004.

223 "to vote on things": Ibid.

223 "the less competent I become": "Oprah Talks to Jon Stewart." *The Oprah Magazine*, June 1, 2005.

223 "it will be an enormous change": Janice Turner, "How Jon Stewart Became the Most Powerful Man on TV." *The Times* (London), October 2, 2010.

223 "as nimbly as I need to": Ibid.

223 "to work this hard": "Oprah Talks to Jon Stewart." *The Oprah Magazine*, June 1, 2005.

224 "the Crypt Keeper at a certain point": Aly Semigran & Josh Horowitz, "Jon Stewart Talks *Death to Smoochy* Sequel at Comedy Awards." *MTV News*, April 10, 2011.

224 "an old guy yelling at the TV": Nikki Finke, "Jon Stewart Says WGA Nixed Side Deal." *Deadline Hollywood*, January 7, 2008.

224 "terrible at a variety of things": "Jon Stewart Juggles TV, Movie Careers." *Orange County Register,* July 9, 1999.

224 "just like it is with soccer": Brian Kilmeade, *The Games Do Count.* New York: HarperCollins, 2008.

224 "I love the Jersey shore": Ed Condran, "Stand-up Comedy Lifts Jon Stewart Out of His *Daily Show* Seat." *The Morning Call,* November 26, 1999.

225 "I've done is try": Ben Domenech, "Jon Stewart: The *SIN* Interview." *Student Information Network (William & Mary),* April 26, 2002.

INDEX

Page numbers in italics indicate photographs